Silverware

Andrew Podnieks

HOCKEY HALL *of* FAME

SILVERWARE

A Fenn Publishing Book / First Published in 2005

Fenn Publishing Company Ltd.
Bolton, Ontario, Canada
L7E 1W2
www.hbfenn.com

Library and Archives Canada Cataloguing in Publication

Podnieks, Andrew
        Silverware : Hockey Hall of Fame / Andrew Podnieks.

ISBN 1-55168-296-6

        1. Hockey—Awards—History.   2. Hockey Hall of Fame.
I. Hockey Hall of Fame   II. Title.
GV847.P63 2005   796.962   C2005-904407-1

Printed in Canada

Silverware

Andrew Podnieks

HOCKEY HALL *of* FAME

Fenn Publishing Company Ltd.

Bolton, Ontario

Also by Andrew Podnieks in the Hockey Hall of Fame Series

Lord Stanley's Cup (2004)
Honoured Members of the Hockey Hall of Fame (2003)

Other Books by Andrew Podnieks

The Lost Season (2005)
The Little Book of Hockey Sweaters (with Rob Hynes, 2005)
2005 IIHF World Championship Media Guide (2005)
The Flames: Celebrating Calgary's Dream Season, 2003-04 (2004)
Players: The Ultimate A-Z Guide of Everyone Who Has Ever Played in the NHL (2003)
The Goal: Bobby Orr and the Most Famous Goal in Stanley Cup History (2003)
A Day in the Life of the Maple Leafs (2002)
Canadian Gold 2002: Making Hockey History (2002)
Kings of the Ice: A History of World Hockey (with others, 2002)
The Essential Blue & White Book: A Toronto Maple Leafs Fact Book (2001)
Hockey's Greatest Teams: Teams, Players, and Plays that Changed the Game (2000)
The NHL All-Star Game: Fifty Years of the Great Tradition (2000)
The Three Stars and Other Selections (with Jefferson Davis, 2000)
The Great One: The Life and Times of Wayne Gretzky (1999)
Hello Hockey Fans From Coast to Coast (with Jefferson Davis, 1999)
Shooting Stars: Photographs from the Portnoy Collection at the Hockey Hall of Fame (1998)
Red, White, and Gold: Canada at the World Junior Championships 1974-1999 (1998)
Portraits of the Game: Classic Photographs from the Turofsky Collection at the Hockey Hall of Fame (1997)
Canada's Olympic Hockey Teams: The Complete History 1920-1998 (1997)
The Blue and White Book 1997: The Most Complete Toronto Maple Leafs Fact Book Ever Published (1996)
The Red Wings Fact Book 1997: The Most Complete Detroit Red Wings Fact Book Ever Published (1996)
The Blue and White Book: The Most Complete Toronto Maple Leafs Fact Book Ever Published (1995)
Return to Glory: The Leafs From Imlach to Fletcher (1995)

Children's Books

The Spectacular Sidney Crosby (2005)
Hockey Heroes: Paul Kariya (2000)
Hockey Heroes: Patrick Roy (1998)

CONTENTS

The Trophies

Active   Retired   One-time   International

JACK RILEY CUP
EAST COAST HOCKEY LEAGUE

1988-89	CAROLINA THUNDERBIRDS
1989-90	GREENSBORO MONARCHS
1990-91	HAMPTON ROADS ADMIRALS
1991-92	HAMPTON ROADS ADMIRALS
1992-93	TOLEDO STORM
1993-94	TOLEDO STORM
1994-95	RICHMOND RENEGADES
1995-96	CHARLOTTE CHECKERS

HOBEY BAKER MEMORIAL AWARD
PRESENTED ANNUALLY TO THE OUTSTANDING COLLEGIATE HOCKEY PLAYER
IN THE UNITED STATES BY THE
DECATHLON ATHLETIC CLUB OF BLOOMINGTON, MINNESOTA

The Trophies

AHA SENIOR CHAMPIONSHIP TROPHY

1891-1898

THE NAME

The trophy name is purely functional, describing the league for which it is competed and the level of play (senior) for which it represents.

THE TROPHY

One of the most important and beautiful hockey trophies in existence, the AHA championship trophy is sterling silver from top to bottom. The base consists of three circles, the largest of which is in the middle to support the rest of the parts. The body of the trophy has the Montreal achievement engraved, and a small, narrow neck leads to a second, more elaborate body which features a detailed hockey scene on one side and the winning rosters for each year on the other. Firm

handles cling to the sides of this portion, making the trophy easy to lift without causing damage. The top has crossed hockey sticks attached to one side, and a lid is decorative more than practical as the inside is not made for drinking.

GENESIS

The precursor to the Stanley Cup, this trophy celebrated the three successive championships achieved by the Montreal AAA, the last of which in 1893 proved a double honour as the team also won the first Stanley Cup.

WINNER

The Montreal AAA team that captured three Eastern championships in succession changed very little, as the engraved names show. Tom Paton, James Stewart, Allan Cameron,

George Low, Alex Kingan, and Alex Irving all were on each team. The Amateur Athletic Association of Montreal began as a cycling club, but in its earliest days the main winter sport was snowshoeing. The AAA was one of the first clubs to organize a formal hockey team, and when the AHA started play in 1886 it was one of the five teams in the league: Montreal Victorias, Montreal Crystals, the AAA, Ottawa Generals, and Quebec Bulldogs. The final of the AAA's three championships was historic because it gave them the first Stanley Cup as well. The team suffered only one loss all year, 4-2 to Ottawa in its first game, but it was internal squabbling that created turmoil at season's end. The Montreal Hockey Club had recently become affiliated with the AAA, and it was that team's players that formed the core of the Cup winners. They were incensed to learn that the winning team was to be called Montreal AAA and not Montreal Hockey Club, and threatened to reject the awarding of the Stanley Cup! Governors of the AAA mollified the players with gifts and begged the players, if nothing else, not to insult the Governor General. They were swayed, and the Montreal AAA became the first official winners of the Stanley Cup.

TODAY

On December 10, 1898, a meeting of AHA executives took place in Montreal that changed the fabric of the game at that time. A vote was held to admit the Ottawa Capitals to the league, and when the motion passed, three teams—Quebec, the Vics, and Ottawa—withdrew from the league and started their own, the Canadian Amateur Hockey League, which in effect killed the AHA and its championship trophy.

(clockwise from far left) A gorgeous etching on the back side of the trophy depicts a typical outdoor hockey scene; the base of the bowl includes the classic crossed hockey sticks; detail of one section of engraving on the lower section of the trophy.

*Originally there were three players on this trophy, two on the
small pedestals on each side of the base and one, wearing
a toque, on the very top!*

STANLEY CUP

1893-PRESENT

THE NAME

The Stanley Cup is named for Lord Stanley, Earl of Derby, Canada's Governor General from 1888 to 1893.

THE TROPHY

Made of sterling silver, the Stanley Cup is the most changed and re-configured of any sports trophy. It began as a simple bowl, and with the addition of a ring beneath the base for every winner it grew long and thin until the late 1940s when it became unmanageable. It was re-designed to its present form, but because of age and change the oldest part on the current Cup dates back only to 1956. The original bowl remains on display at the Hockey Hall of Fame to ensure its safety.

GENESIS

During his five years in Canada, Lord Stanley and his family became huge fans of Canada's winter pastime. His daughter, Isobel, played with the ladies at Rideau Hall, and his sons were part of the pioneering Rideau Rebels hockey team that played the game for sportsmanship, social value, and competitive enjoyment. Toward the end of his term as Governor General, Lord Stanley decided that he would donate a trophy to Canada. The official announcement came at a banquet to honour the 1892 hockey champions of the east, in Ottawa, on March 18, 1892. In a letter he had written for the gathering and read in his absence by Lord Kilcoursie, Stanley wrote:

"I have for some time past been thinking that it would be a good thing if there were a challenge cup which should be held from year to year by the champion hockey team in the Dominion.

There does not appear to be any such outward and visible sign of championship at present, and considering the general interest which the matches now elicit, and the importance of having the game played fairly and under rules generally recognized, I am willing to give a cup which shall be held from year to year by the winning team.

It would be worth considering whether they could not be arranged so that each team would play once at home and once at the place where their opponents hail from."

FIRST WINNER

The Montreal AAA (Amateur Athletic Association) were inaugural winners of the Stanley Cup by virtue of winning the Amateur Hockey Association championship, a five-team league that also included the Ottawa Generals, Montreal Crystals, Montreal Victorias, and the Quebec Hockey Club. Teams played eight games during the season, and the Montreal AAA's 7-1 record was one win better than Ottawa's 6-2 mark.

CHAMPIONS' HISTORY

The Stanley Cup has become the most important trophy in the world of hockey. It began, as per Lord Stanley's wishes, as a trophy for amateur competition, but over time it came to represent professional play because—also in keeping with his wishes—the best team in Canada soon had paid players on it. As the game expanded to include teams from the United States, the trophy moved south occasionally, again because sometimes the best team played south of the border. The Stanley Cup has been awarded annually since 1893, with the lone exceptions of 1919 when a flu pandemic in Seattle forced the postponement of the Seattle Metropolitans-Montreal Canadiens final and the 2004-05 season when a lockout cancelled play for the entire season. To accommodate the growing list of winners, the Cup underwent several redesigns as it became clear during the 1940s that ring after ring could not be added indefinitely to the base of the original bowl. Today, the core of the Cup is its five barrel rings, each of which can hold 13 winners. The Hockey Hall of Fame now ensures that the Cup will forever retain its current shape by a brilliant solution. When the bottom ring is filled, the top ring is removed and displayed in the Hall. The other rings are moved up, and an empty ring is fitted to the bottom of the Cup to allow for 13 more winners.

TODAY

The Cup is unquestionably the most famous and identifiable sports trophy in the world, more popular, in fact, than the game itself! Players on the winning team are now allowed to keep the trophy for a day, and with the influx of international players to the NHL this has meant the Cup has traveled the world over, from dozens of towns and cities across Canada, to Alaska, Russia, and throughout Europe.

The engraving (clockwise from far left) clearly indicates Lord Stanley's original intent for his trophy, to be fought for by any and all worthy comers; detail of one year's Cup champions; one side of the bowl features Lord Stanley's name.

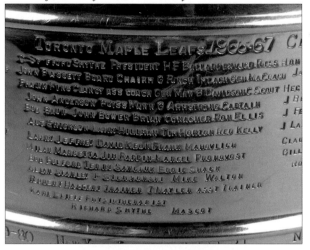

With the engraving of the champion Tampa Bay Lightning for 2003-04, the bottom barrel of the Stanley Cup is now full. When the '05-'06 winners' names are stamped, the top rung must first be removed, the others slid up, and a new empty ring put into place at the bottom.

CAHL CHAMPIONSHIP TROPHY

1898-1905

THE NAME

The Canadian Amateur Hockey League was the premier league in Canada at the turn of the 20th century.

THE TROPHY

Resembling an ornate punch bowl, this trophy is squat and fat and looks more practical than most hockey trophies. It sits on a wood base which has small shields nailed into its side with the names of the winning teams, but it's the bowl itself that shines in this case. The rim is rippled and clovered, the side decorated with flowers, fruits, and ribbons. The inside is smooth and clearly has seen its contents filled for celebration!

GENESIS

The CAHL started in 1898-99, taking over the role of the AHA (Amateur Hockey Association) from the previous season. The CAHL featured five teams: the Montreal Shamrocks, Montreal Victorias, Ottawa Hockey Club, Montreal AAA (sometimes called the Montreal Hockey Club), and Quebec Hockey Club. This trophy was awarded to the winner of the regular season play which, in its first season, was an eight-game season that saw each team play every other twice (one home, one away).

FIRST WINNER

The Shamrocks finished in first place by virtue of their 7-1 record, one win better than the second place Victorias. That margin of victory was the result of their classic game on the second-last day of the season, March 1, 1899, when the Shamrocks beat the Vics 1-0. The game was played before a sellout crowd of 8,000, and the only goal of the game went to Harry Trihey who led the league with 19 goals in seven

games. Other star players on the team included Art Farrell, Jack Brannen, and Fred Scanlan. The Shamrocks went on to capture the Stanley Cup just two weeks later, defeating Queen's University 6-2 in a one-game challenge. Trihey scored a hat trick in that game, and Farrell had two goals to lead the team to its first Cup.

CHAMPIONS' HISTORY

The Shamrocks repeated as league and Stanley Cup champions the following season thanks again to the goalscoring of Trihey and Farrell. Again they suffered only one loss all year, 4-3 to Quebec on the final day of the season when their victory was already assured. The Montreal AAA finished two wins behind at 5-2. In 1901, Ottawa was the class of the league, sporting a 7-0-1 record and easily topping the second-place Victorias (4-3-1). During the season, the Shamrocks lost the Cup to the Winnipeg Victorias in a two-game series and Ottawa didn't have a chance to challenge before the season ended. Unluckily, they lost the next CAHL season of play to the Montreal AAA who then traveled to Winnipeg and beat the Vics 2-1 in the final game of a best-of-three series. Ottawa won a measure of revenge the following year. It tied the Montreal Vics atop the standings for the CAHL championship, so the two-game playoff also became a fight for the Stanley Cup because earlier in the year the AAA had defeated Winnipeg again to keep the Cup in the east for the rest of the season. Ottawa and the Montreal Vics tied 1-1 in the first game, but in game two the Silver Seven, as they became known, swamped Montreal 8-0 to win both the CAHL trophy and the Stanley Cup. In 1903-04., it was Quebec, which had a record of 0-8 in the league's first year of play, that now won the CAHL trophy with a 7-1 record, but during the year Ottawa withdrew from the CAHL and entered the new Federal Amateur Hockey League

(FAHL), taking with it the right to play for the Stanley Cup. So, despite the win, Quebec could not challenge Ottawa for the Cup and the Silver Seven instead defeated a series of other teams to remain in possession of the ultimate prize. Similarly, the Montreal Vics won the next year, compiling a 9-1 record on the strength of Russell Bowie and Russell Blair, who finished 1-2 in scoring with 26 and 19 goals, respectively. But it was Ottawa in the FAHL that continued to play for the Stanley Cup, shutting out the CAHL from the competition.

TODAY

On December 11, 1905, executives from the CAHL met with their counterparts of the Federal league and decided to amalgamate into one strong and unified organization. Thus was born the Eastern Canada Amateur Hockey Association (ECAHA). As a result, the CAHL championship trophy was retired and a new trophy introduced for the champions of the new league.

(clockwise from far left) Detail of the engraving to indicate the trophy's significance; a wreath, symbolic of victory, is entwined among crossed sticks; this scene appears on the back side of the bowl.

Leagues in the east fought relentlessly with each other for players and a place in the hockey world. The result was a frequent shuffling of team names, league affiliations, and trophy relevance which resulted in this beautiful mug lasting just seven seasons.

JOHN ROSS ROBERTSON CUP

1899-PRESENT

THE NAME

Most notably a journalist, Robertson worked for the Globe before founding the Evening Telegram in 1876. It quickly became the most influential and important newspaper of the day. Through his successes, he contributed generously to the building of the Hospital for Sick Children, and he later published "Landmarks of Toronto," a six-volume work on the city's history and key buildings and people that remains the finest collection published on that city.

THE TROPHY

Crafted by the Queen's jewelers and silversmiths in London, England, the trophy is made of sterling silver from Canada and lined with Canadian gold. The bowl is decorated in bas relief with lions and masks, but the most striking characteristic is the three leopard handles. The ebony plinth has Hogarth shields on it to recognize winning teams.

GENESIS

Robertson was a great believer in the power of sports to develop character and manliness, and to this end he was heavily involved in hockey. He was one of the first presidents of the Ontario Hockey Association and in that capacity

donated three trophies bearing his name to be awarded to the provincial champions in senior, intermediate, and junior competition in Ontario. He donated this senior trophy, the oldest of the triumvirate, to the OHA on December 3, 1898.

FIRST WINNER

Queen's University in Kingston, Ontario, won the first competition for this senior trophy in 1899. The names of the players are engraved on the shield for that year: R. Hiscock, G. Curtis, R. Meryll, J.J. Hart, G.F. Danton, F.F. Carr-Harris, and K. Walkem.

CHAMPIONS' HISTORY

The delightful shields with team and player names reveal a wealth of hockey history. Famous names dot the trophy, from Syl Apps (Hamilton Tigers, 1936) to Darryl Sly (1974,

Barrie) to Harry Sinden (1959, Barrie). The Toronto Granites are on here for 1922 and 1923, and the next year they went to the Olympics and came home with gold for Canada. In the early days, many players from these teams went on to great success in the NHL; in later years, as senior and amateur hockey slipped into the background, they went from great success to senior hockey toward the end of their careers. Either way, the senior Ontario Robertson Cup is one of the most prestigious trophies in provincial hockey.

TODAY

The Aylmer Blues won the 2004-05 Robertson Trophy, defeating Dundas 4-1 in the final stage of the Ontario Senior AAA playoffs (it is now sometimes called Ontario Major League Hockey). This gave the Blues the right to go north to play the Thunder Bay Bombers in a best-of-three series, the winner claiming the Renwick Cup and earning the right to go to the Allan Cup finals (Thunder Bay received this special status because teams couldn't afford to travel so far north to play in league action). Incredibly, Thunder Bay swept the series by scores of 1-0 and 5-3 to advance to the Allan Cup, and once there they didn't waste the opportunity, capturing the national senior amateur championship by beating the Montmagny Sentinelles 4-3 in the finals.

(left) Frontal view of the lion-handle of the cup; (middle top) detail of the lion's menacing head; (middle bottom) the plaque for the first winners, from Queen's University in 1899; (right) full profile of the elaborate handle.

Dating to the end of the 19th century, this senior trophy is one of three given by John Ross Robertson for the champions of Ontario in the three levels of serious amateur hockey: junior, intermediate, senior.

TROPHY TO DAN BAIN

1902

THE NAME

A commemorative trophy honouring Dan Bain's career in hockey, this piece of hardware has no specific name.

THE TROPHY

At 8" in height, this is one of the smaller trophies in the Hockey Hall of Fame's collection, yet it is ornate nonetheless. The base, stem, and bowl are all handsomely inlaid, the latter further engraved with the dedication: "D.H. (Dan) Bain, captain of Winnipeg Victoria Senior Hockey Team, 1895-1902"

GENESIS

Dan Bain was named Canada's athlete of the last half of the 19th century. No wonder! In 1887, at the age of 13, he won a provincial roller skating contest in Manitoba. At 17, he was a champion gymnast in Winnipeg. Soon after, he was one-mile bike racing winner for three years running (1894-96), and in 1903, after his outstanding hockey career, he was Canada's trap shooting champion.

Bain won tournaments in golf and lacrosse, and when he was in his late forties he took up figure skating—and promptly won tournaments. By the time he retired in 1930 from active competition, his place in Canadian history was set. Hockey fans knew him for his eight years as captain of the Winnipeg Victorias, where he awed fans with his skating and stickhandling abilities. Not the slimmest man to play, he was nonetheless graceful and very fast, and many of his contem

poraries considered him the finest player around. Bain led the Vics to three Stanley Cups, the first in 1896 when he scored the Cup-winning goal in a 2-0 victory over the Montreal Victorias. Five years later, Bain did it again, scoring the winner in overtime of a 2-1 win over the Montreal Shamrocks. The next year, 1902, the Vics defeated Toronto Wellingtons in a two-game challenge to defend their championship, after which Bain retired. He was an inaugural inductee to the Hockey Hall of Fame and later into Canada's Sports Hall of Fame.

In honour of his glorious career with stick and puck, he was presented this tiny, perfect trophy.

Detail from the side of the cup commemorating Dan Bain's spectacular hockey career.

Without the engraving, one might almost think this was a chalice taken right from the altar at St. Peter's Basilica such is the decorative beauty and immaculate proportion of this honour bestowed upon Dan Bain, Canadian hockey star from the turn of the 20th century.

QUEEN'S CUP

THE NAME

The trophy is simply named after Queen's University, which presented this beautiful silver cup to the Canadian Intercollegiate Hockey Union in February 1903.

THE TROPHY

All that is left of the Queen's Cup today is the gorgeous bowl. Made of sterling, it is delicate from age and slightly bent and dented from wear and tear. All winners between 1933 and 1995 are engraved on the bowl (except 1940-45 when the war prevented its being competed for and 1990-92 and '93-'94 for which there are spaces but engravings were never made). The rim of the bowl is accented by beautiful detail all the way around, making this one of the more ornate bowls in the collection. The original base, missing here, continues to be used on the new replica trophy introduced in 1999.

GENESIS

While never as glamourous as other hockey leagues and championships in Canada, university level hockey developed almost as quickly as the professional game and from hockey's formal invention in 1875 in Montreal (by McGill University students) to today its annual championship is an important

part of the university athletic calendar. The Queen's Cup has been awarded every year since 1903 with the exception of the war years. When it was first presented, only teams from Ontario and Quebec were part of the Union. In 1910, teams from the Maritime Inter-Collegiate Athletic Association joined the competition, and in 1919 Western Canadian Intercollegiate Athletic Union teams signed up. In 1963, all Canadian universities were part of a CIAU that competed regionally to determine champions to play a national championship, the winners receiving the University Cup. Through all these developments, the Queen's Cup remained an Ontario-Quebec prize until 1971 when Quebec universities (with the exception of their hockey teams) left the O-QAA (Ontario-Quebec Athletic Association), thus allowing Ontario to rename its league the OUAA (Ontario Universities Athletic Association), where the Queen's Cup remains in competition.

FIRST WINNER

McGill University won the inaugural Queen's Cup in January 1903. Little is known about the team, although the lineup included the scoring star Doc Wright, as well as captain W. Evans, Jack Lash, A.B. Wright, Jakey Brown, W.A. Gilbert, Jack McLean, W.G. Wood, and Dillabough.

CHAMPIONS' HISTORY

One of the oldest hockey trophies competed for annually, the Queen's Cup was not handed out during most of the war years (1940-45). The University of Toronto has won it more

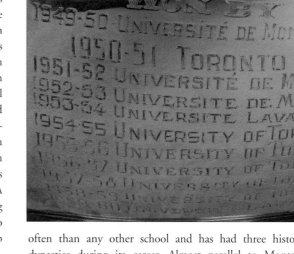

often than any other school and has had three historic dynasties during its career. Almost parallel to Montreal Canadiens' five Stanley Cups in succession, the U of T Blues won the provincial/regional championship from 1954-59. They bettered that a decade later, winning eight successive Queen's Cups from 1965 to 1973, and between '74 and '84 they won five more times. The only other university to have anywhere near this success was McGill. The Redmen won six in a row (1933-39). York University had a string of four in a row (1984-88). The last names on the Cup are for the University of Western Ontario, winners in 1994-95.

TODAY

Because of the lack of organized leagues at the university level outside of eastern Canada, the Queen's Cup used to symbolize national supremacy as well. But with the introduction of the University Cup in 1961, the Queen's Cup became fully a regional trophy only. Nonetheless, the champions of Ontario still receive the Queen's Cup to this day.

(left) Detail of the engraving on the side of the bowl;
(top) some of the winners' names as they appear on the bowl;
(above) McGill won the trophy six consecutive times (1933-39).

Canadian university hockey used to produce more than its fair share of hockey stars, and for more than a century the Queen's Cup has remained the Stanley Cup for champions at that level.

ARENA CUP

1905-1909

THE NAME

Big, beautiful, ornate, and decorative, the Arena Cup is one of the few major trophies without eponymous reference, instead gaining its name simply from the place in which hockey is played, that is, a hockey arena.

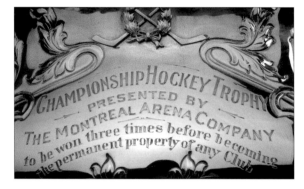

THE TROPHY

One of the showpieces of the Hockey Hall of Fame's collection, the Arena Cup features a large open bowl with silver hockey players on opposite sides, where handles might normally be placed. It is so named because it was a gift of the Montreal Arena Company and intended for full possession by any team that won three straight championships. The bowl sits on a round wood base, black, and only slightly wider than the base of the silver bowl itself. On it are three shields memorializing winners.

GENESIS

The early 1900s were a time of radical change as hockey cities fought to forge unions and rivalries, players sought professional status so they could be paid to play, and leagues competed for the inclusion of various teams. In December 1905, the Canadian Amateur Hockey League (CAHL) and the Federal Amateur Hockey League combined to form the Eastern Canada Amateur Hockey Association, consisting of four CAHL teams—Shamrocks, Montreal, Quebec, and Victorias—and two from the Federal league, Ottawa and the Wanderers, thereby excluding two teams from the CAHL (Westmount and Nationals) and three more from the FAHL (Brockville, Cornwall, and Montagnards). As a result of the amalgamation, the new ECAHA needed a championship trophy for the first place team in league competition, and so the Arena Cup was born.

FIRST WINNER

The Ottawa Silver Seven won the first Arena Cup. Both the Silver Seven and Wanderers finished in a tie for first place with identical 9-1 records, each team's only loss coming against the other, but Ottawa having scored more goals. Ottawa was led by first-year star Harry Smith who led the league with 31 goals in just eight games, and Frank McGee who had 28 goals in just seven games. Ottawa averaged nearly two goals a game more than the next highest-scoring team, the Victorias, but in the Stanley Cup series they were defeated by the Wanderers 12-10 in a two-game, total goals series.

CHAMPIONS' HISTORY

The ECAHA lasted only two more years before changing its name to ECHA, dropping the word "amateur" to reflect the growing trend by teams to contracting professionals to play the game. The Wanderers won the league championship in both 1907 and '08, and continued to win the Stanley Cup as well. In 1907, they boasted a perfect 10-0 record, and the year after they were 8-2. In the Stanley Cup challenge series, they defeated the Kenora Thistles, Ottawa Victorias, Winnipeg Maple Leafs, a team from Toronto, and then the Edmonton Eskimos in succession, establishing themselves as one of the greatest pre-NHL teams. To honour this run of sensational victories, the ECHA gave Wanderers' captain Cecil Blachford the Arena Cup in recognition of his leadership for all Arena and Stanley Cup teams during this era.

TODAY

The ECHA lasted only until 1909 when the league, trying the expel the Wanderers, reformed under the name Canadian Hockey Association. As a result, the Arena Cup was abandoned, and for decades has been the property of the Hockey Hall of Fame, a sumptuous memento from a great era of hockey in eastern Canada.

(top left) Although called the Arena Cup, the formal name appears on the side of the bowl; (above) a plaque honouring one of the three winners; (right) players replace handles on either side of the bowl.

This beautiful trophy lasted only a few short years after which the league it represented, the ECAHA, was replaced by the ECHA, rendering the trophy redundant. To honour his accomplishments with the team, Wanderers' great Cecil Blachford was given it at the end of his career.

KENORA THISTLES MUG TO JOE HALL

1907

THE NAME

This commemorative mug was given to Joe Hall shortly after the Kenora Thistles won the Stanley Cup in January 1907.

THE TROPHY

This is a true mug. Less than a foot high and perfectly capable of holding a beer, this sterling silver honour is as practical as it is beautiful. Its shapely design resembles the torso (fat at the top, receding in the middle, fatter again at the bottom) and has two simple handles. The engraving makes clear Hall's contributions to the Cup run were much appreciated by the citizenry of Kenora.

GENESIS

Joe Hall had played the 1906-07 season in Brandon, but he was recruited by the Thistles, along with Art Ross and Roxy Beaudro, for the Cup challenge series for a then staggering fee of $1,000.

FIRST WINNER

Kenora travelled to Montreal and defeated the Wanderers 12-8 in a two-game, total-goals series that was perhaps the greatest upset in Cup history. It became the smallest town by far to win the Cup, and it did so in dramatic fashion. The Thistles won the first game 4-2, Tom Phillips scoring all goals for Kenora. In the deciding game it was Tom Hooper who played the hero. He scored five goals (Phillips had two of the other three) to power the Thistles to victory. The game had been tied 6-6 in the second half when Beaudro scored to give the Thistles that needed cushion, and goaltender Eddie Geroux was brilliant in fending off a potent Wanderers' offense that included Pud Glass, Ernie Russell, and Cecil Blachford.

Joe Hall, often called "Bad" Joe Hall or "Mean" Joe Hall, went on to have a Hall of Fame career. He moved east in 1907 to play in Montreal, and in 1910 he began a successful, seven-year run with the Quebec Bulldogs, winning the Cup in 1912 and 1913. He played in the NHL with the Montreal Canadiens for the first two years of the league's existence (1917-19), but he died of influenza during the 1919 Stanley Cup finals in Seattle, the year the series was cancelled and the Cup not awarded because of the pandemic that swept the city and lay low most players on both teams (though Hall was the only player to die from the sickness).

CHAMPIONS' HISTORY

Although Kenora was the smallest town to win the Cup, its achievement became somewhat dubious when, just 63 days later, it lost the Cup, thus setting a record for shortest reign as Cup champions. To qualify for the re-match, the Wanderers first had to win the ECAHA championship, which they did by finishing in first place with a perfect 10-0-0 record, ahead of second place Ottawa. The Wanderers then challenged the Thistles, the games now being played out west, but ice conditions were bad in Kenora and the games were transferred to nearby Winnipeg. The visitors dominated the first game and cruised to a 7-2 win, but in game two the Thistles prevailed, 6-5. However, because this was a total-goals series, the Wanderers won 12-8 on aggregate and took the Cup right back to Montreal, scarcely two months after losing it! Art Ross was no longer with the Thistles, who recruited Alf Smith and Harry Westwick as ringers, but they were no match for Ernie Russell who scored five of Montreal's dozen goals in the series.

TODAY

The town of Kenora is but a footnote in early Stanley Cup history. It never came close to competing for the Cup again, but it remains the smallest city ever to win Lord Stanley's Cup. Hall, meanwhile, was inducted into the Hockey Hall of Fame in 1961 for a spectacular 14-year professional career that ended too soon.

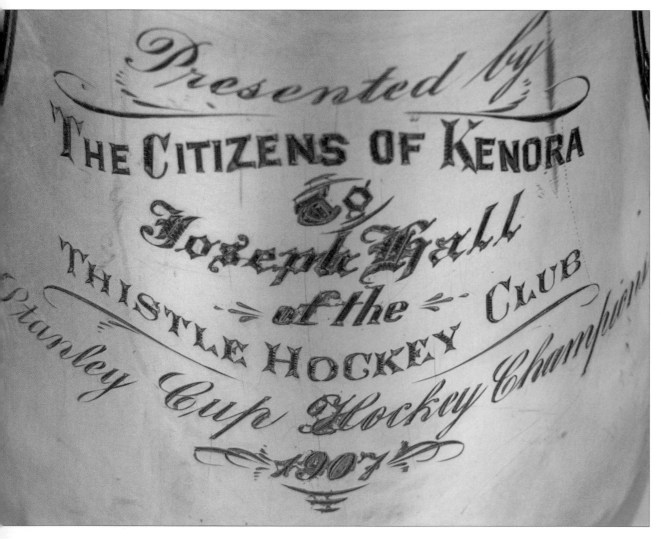

Presented by The Citizens of Kenora to Joseph Hall of the Thistle Hockey Club Stanley Cup Hockey Champions 1907

Detail of the engraving on the mug from the people of Kenora to Joe Hall who helped bring the Stanley Cup to their small town.

Presented by
THE CITIZENS OF KENORA
to
Joseph Hall
of the
THISTLE HOCKEY CLUB
Stanley Cup Hockey Champions
1907

Simple, elegant, and handsome, this sterling silver mug was cherished by Hall from the time he was given it in 1907 to his untimely death during the 1919 Stanley Cup playoffs when virtually the entire Montreal team suffered from influenza.

MONTREAL WANDERERS MUG

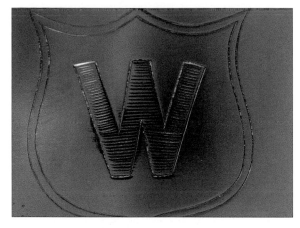

1907

THE NAME

This mug was presented to the Wanderers hockey club by George Simpson following the team's Stanley Cup victory in March 1907 to reclaim from Kenora what it had lost two months earlier.

THE TROPHY

This personal championship trophy, given to the Wanderers in honour of their Stanley Cup victory, is a gold and slightly more elaborate version of what Joe Hall was given by the people of Kenora. It is slightly taller and twice as fat and has three handles to give it more a sense of celebration and symbol than of practical use. Again, the inscription records for history the important events pertaining to its being presented.

GENESIS

In January 1907, the Kenora Thistles traveled to Montreal where they shocked the easterners with 4-2 and 8-6 victories to walk away with the Cup. The Wanderers then started their ECAHA league season, won first place, and earned the right to challenge the Thistles for the Cup again.

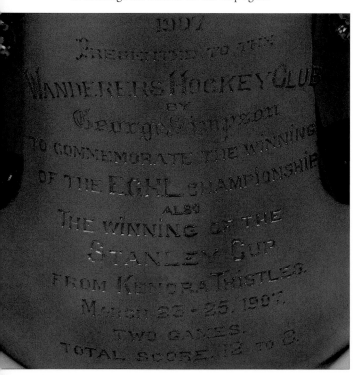

FIRST WINNER

By rights, this Wanderers team never should have lost the Cup to the upstarts from Kenora in the first place, so superior were their players to Kenora's. They earned revenge by going through the ECAHA season undefeated, led by goalie Riley Hern who was the league's best, by a long shot. The team had plenty of firepower with Ernie Russell scoring 42 goals in nine league games, including two, eight-goal games. Hod Stuart represented an example of the changing times in the league because he was being paid to play, one of a growing number of professionals changing the once amateur-only ECAHA league into what would soon be a pros-only operation. Nonetheless, they had great difficulty winning the Cup back. They won the first game but lost the second, and it was only the margins of the scores that gave the Wanderers the Cup based on total goals (12-8).

CHAMPIONS' HISTORY

The Wanderers won the Cup eight times over a four-year period (1906-10), the result of both league play and successful Cup defence from challenges by other top teams in Canada. They won for the first time in March 1906 by defeating Ottawa in an ECAHA playoff to break a tie in the standings. In December of that year they thrashed New Glasgow in a two-game, total-goals challenge, 17-5, and a few months later they beat the Thistles. In the first three months of 1908, the Wanderers won three successive challenges—from Ottawa Victorias, Winnipeg Maple Leafs, and Toronto Trolley Leaguers—and at the end of the year they beat the Edmonton Eskimos in another challenge. The Wanderers won for the last time in March 1910 as a result of their first-place finish in the NHA, and they went on to beat Berlin 7-3 in a one-game challenge. The Wanderers ceased operations after five games of NHL play in December 1917 when their arena burned down and they chose to disband rather than find a new home.

TODAY

That 1907 victory by the Wanderers holds one of the most important places in Cup history. The results of those games, and the complete team roster, were engraved into the bottom of the bowl of the Cup itself, taking up the entire area and ensuring its place in perpetuity not only among the winners but among the various incarnations of the Cup has undergone in the last century or more.

(left) Inscription detailing the accomplishments of the 1907 Montreal Wanderers; (middle) the simple crest for the team; (above) the roster of the team that wrested the Cup from the Kenora Thistles.

One of the unique features of this mug is that is has three handles instead of the traditional two. Like a mini Stanley Cup, it also has engraved on it the team name and complete roster of the players who lost the Cup to Kenora and then regained it just a few weeks later in early 1907.

ALLAN CUP

1909-PRESENT

THE NAME

The eponymous origin of this trophy comes from Sir Montagu Allan, a wealthy Montreal lawyer and famed horse breeder whose horses had won the Queen's Plate. He was knighted in 1904 and received the CVO (Commander of the Royal Victorian Order) three years later.

THE TROPHY

Historically the most important trophy in Canada after the Stanley Cup, the Allan Cup looks as spectacular as ever in the 21st century as it did when it was first competed for. The trophy itself is an elaborate design with a unique, funnel-like stem that connects the base to the bulbous top. That base features small, multi-pointed maple leafs into which are engraved the names of the earliest winners of the trophy. The engraving in the body of the trophy calls this a "perpetual challenge trophy." On the other side, this sterling silver cup includes a detailed vignette with the trophy's dedication: "In honour of the hockey players who served overseas in the Great War 1914-18." The wood base is equally unique. Slightly wider than the base of the trophy, it is decorated with silver maple leaves consistent with what is on the sterling bowl itself, the continuation of winning names decorating the black base which is not yet full.

GENESIS

When Lord Stanley donated his trophy to the people of Canada in 1892, the Stanley Cup almost immediately became the most important hockey trophy in the country. But, by the early 1900s, the leagues which contested the Cup had changed from amateur to professional, leaving the unpaid ranks without a championship trophy. Sir Montagu Allan stepped in and ordered a trophy made in his name, to be given annually to the best amateur team in the land. When the Canadian Amateur Hockey Association (CAHA) was formed in 1914, it adopted the Allan Cup as its own, and although it became a Senior AAA trophy in 1984, it still repersents amateur supremacy in Canada.

FIRST WINNER

It cannot be denied that the Ottawa Cliffsides were the first winners of the Allan Cup, even though the trophy had not been completed in time for a formal presentation after victory. However, theirs was likeliest the shortest celebration in hockey history, for just a few days later they were challenged by Queen's University and lost! The elapsed time was just ten days, from March 6-16, 1909, between victory and defeat. In the challenge game, the score was tied 4-4 after regulation time and referee Blair Russell, after consulting the rule book, decreed that the teams must play until a victor had been decided. Some 14 minutes later, Queen's scored to wrest the Allan Cup from the Cliffsides.

CHAMPIONS' HISTORY

Up through the 1950s, the Allan Cup was every bit as important and popular as the Stanley Cup among Canadian hockey fans. Today, it seems ludicrous to compare the two, but in its day the Allan Cup was as proud a win as Lord Stanley's bowl. In large measure this was because international hockey was competed at the amateur level, so from 1920 until 1976 only amateur players could compete in the Olympics and World Championships. For much of that time the CAHA named the Allan Cup winners at the team to represent Canada internationally, from the Winnipeg Falcons in 1920 to the Kitchener-Waterloo Dutchmen in 1955. The prestige of winning gold for Canada, which largely won uncontested in those years, was unparalleled. Perhaps the greatest Allan Cup teams, though, were the two Ottawa entries that won during World War II, the RCAF team of 1942 and the Commandos team a year later. The former featured the great forward line from Boston of Milt Schmidt-Woody Dumart-Bobby Bauer, which had left the Bruins to join Canada's war efforts. The latter had Sugar Jim Henry in goal, as well as Neil and Max Colville, Bingo Kampman, Ken Reardon, and Alex Shibicky among others, all stars of the NHL.

TODAY

Although senior hockey does not enjoy the same prestige it once did, the Allan Cup approaches its 100th anniversary still proud and strong and it is still competed for every spring. St. Georges Garaga won in 2004, repeating its success of two years earlier, but two recent dynasties stand out. The Warroad Lakers became the first team ever to win three in a row (1993-96) and the Thunder Bay Twins won four times in a six-year period (1983-89), the two most dominant teams in trophy history. The champions for 2004-05 were the Thunder Bay Bombers.

(above and below) Details from the base of the Allan Cup in which team winners are engraved on small, silver maple leaf plaques.

One of the oldest and most important trophies in all of hockey, the Allan Cup features that age-old symbol of Canada—the maple leaf—into which are engraved the names of winning teams. The earliest silver leaves are attached to a small branch that enriches the arboreal feel to the imagery.

O'BRIEN TROPHY

admitted to the Eastern Canada Hockey League, in 1909. The ECHL, however, refused his application, so O'Brien formed his own league, the National Hockey Association (NHA), which started out with seven teams, four of which he owned—the Creamery Kings and teams from Cobalt and Haileybury as well as the Montreal Wanderers. Other teams included a Montreal team made up solely of French players, called the Montreal Canadiens, as well as the Montreal Shamrocks and a team from Ottawa. O'Brien crafted a championship trophy bearing his name using silver from one of his mines. Three seasons later, he sold three of the teams, his Renfrew Stanley Cup dreams never having materialized.

FIRST WINNER

The Montreal Wanderers finished atop the NHA standings with an 11-1-0 record, their only loss coming early in the season to Haileybury. Riley Hern was the team's goalie, and Harry Hyland, with 20 goals in eleven games, was the Wanderers' scoring star. The Wanderers also won the Stanley Cup that 1909-10 season when they successfully accepted a challenge from a team in Berlin (Kitchener), Ontario. The Wanderers won the one-game playdown 7-3, Ernie Russell (four goals) and Harry Hyland (three) doing all the damage for the winners.

THE NAME

Senator Michael J. O'Brien made his name and fortune in Renfrew, Ontario, in logging, mining, and other natural resources business interests. In 1918 he became a senator on the appointment of Prime Minister Robert Borden.

THE TROPHY

One of the most beautiful pieces of hockey trophy history, the O'Brien is spectacular no matter from which angle it is admired. The bowl on top is flat and wide brimmed, like an upside-down pot top, and the rest is made of solid wood that gives it the bulk of its weight (more than 45 lbs.). There are four parts to the base: the first two hold plaques upon which winning teams' names are engraved and between which are placed laurel wreaths; the third is a rounded tier almost as wide with two highly detailed hockey scenes that are the sport's versions of hieroglyphs; and, the top is a small square that supports the bowl and which contains the dedication.

GENESIS

Among the many ambitions of M.J. O'Brien was to bring the Stanley Cup to his hometown of Renfrew. To this end, he sought to have his hockey team, the Renfrew Creamery Kings,

CHAMPIONS' HISTORY

The O'Brien Trophy remained symbolic of NHA regular-season champions until 1917 when that league became the NHL. The new league continued to use it as an award for the first place team until 1924 when it was replaced by the Prince of Wales Trophy. After lying inactive for four years, the O'Brien was revived in 1928 when the NHL had two divisions, the trophy now going to the first-place team of the Canadian Division. In 1939, when the league reverted to a one-division format, the O'Brien Trophy was given to the second-place team at the end of the regular season. It was last awarded for the 1949-50 season when the Montreal Canadiens won it. In the NHA, Ottawa, Quebec, and the Canadiens all won it twice, and in the NHL it was the Leafs who won it most—nine times in all (the Canadiens won it seven times).

TODAY

The O'Brien Trophy has long been a part of the Hockey Hall of Fame's inventory of silverware, but in 1991 it made an historic return to its home for the Renfrew Lumber Baron Summer Festival, its first trip to O'Brien's hometown since its unveiling more than 80 years previous.

(top left) The plaque attached to the wood base beneath the bowl; (above) details from the side and base of the trophy; (below) bronze relief depicting a traditional hockey scene with many players fighting for the puck.

Out of circulation for more than half a century, the O'Brien Trophy remains among the most stunning hockey awards ever created. The players rise out of the bronze and with Herculean grace play hockey and almost support the bowl on top. Below, the plaques honouring winning teams look like something recovered from a Grecian archaeological site.

FRANK FOYSTON'S PCHA MVP TROPHY

1917

THE NAME

This mug was given to Frank Foyston for his outstanding contributions to his Seattle Metropolitans team at the conclusion of the 1916-17 season.

THE TROPHY

An odd mix of styles, this award to Frank Foyston has a wood base shaped like a large knob. It supports a beautiful mug with horn-like handles that span the length of the mug. The inscription adorns one side of the mug, but the other side is plain. The rim at the top is petal-shaped.

GENESIS

The PCHA first came into being in 1911, formed by the Patrick brothers, Frank and Lester, to compete for players with the National Hockey Association (NHA). In its first year, the PCHA consisted of only three teams: New Westminster Royals, Vancouver Millionaires, and Victoria Aristocrats. In its fourth year, the Royals were replaced by a team from the United States, the Portland Rosebuds, for the 1914-15 season. In March 1916, the Rosebuds faced the Montreal Canadiens in a best-of-five Stanley Cup challenge, the Habs winning by the narrowest of margins, 2-1, in the fifth and final game. The next year, the Seattle Metropolitans joined the PCHA, which now had two Canadian and two American teams. The "Mets" won the league title, and in the Stanley Cup playoffs they beat the Canadiens in four games to become the first American team to win Lord Stanley's Canadian prize. Key to the victory was Frank Foyston who scored seven times in that series.

WINNER

One of the game's early-20th century stars, Foyston won the Stanley Cup three times, each with a different team. The Minesing, Ontario, native began his pro career with the Toronto Blueshirts in the NHA in 1912, leading that team to his first Cup just two years later. But like many players from this era, Foyston left the east and signed on to play in the PCHA, in his case with Seattle, early into the '15-'16 season. By the end of the next season, he had led the Metropolitans to an historic Cup victory, scoring four goals in seven games and leading the team through inspiration as much as offense. His was a choppy skating stride, deceiving and effective but not anything like the evident blazing speed or skill of Cyclone Taylor or Frank McGee. For this wonderful season, sportswriters covering the PCHA awarded Foyston the mug for best all round player in the game, a tribute not just to his offense but also his leadership, defensive abilities, and overall team play, a trophy similar to, for instance, the modern NHL's Frank Selke Trophy. Two years later, in the spring of 1919, he led the Mets in the Stanley Cup finals series against Montreal by scoring nine goals in just four games, but the series had to be cancelled when the Canadiens' Joe Hall died of the flu and most other players were hospitalized with the virus. In all, Foyston played in Seattle for nine years until the team folded, and then traveled north to Victoria where, in his first season, 1924-25, he took the Cougars to a Stanley Cup victory, the last time a non-NHL team won the trophy. He then joined the Detroit Cougars, an expansion team into the NHL in 1926, when that team bought and recruited most of the Cougars to join the NHL. Officially, Foyston played just 64 NHL games—none in the playoffs—but by the time he retired in 1930 he had long ago established himself as one of the greatest players of his era. He was inducted into the Hockey Hall of Fame in 1958.

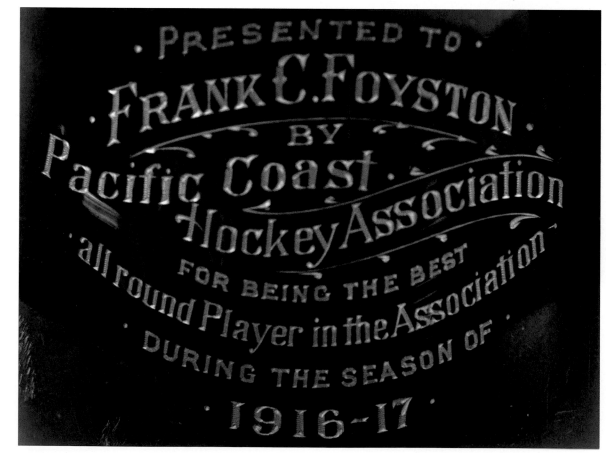

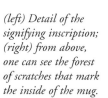

(left) Detail of the signifying inscription; (right) from above, one can see the forest of scratches that mark the inside of the mug.

PRESENTED TO
FRANK E. FOYSTON
BY
Pacific Coast
Hockey Association
FOR BEING THE BEST AND
Player in the Association
DURING THE SEASON OF
1916-17

A mug as trophy always looks part aesthetic, part functional, but in this case the mug is mounted on a wood base to dispel any sense that this might have been used for drink as well. This is sheer, lovely ornament.

MEMORIAL CUP

THE NAME

Named in honour of the players who gave their lives during World War I, the Memorial Cup has been in competition since 1919.

THE TROPHY

The ornate bowl is unusual for its four feet. It sits upon a small, round base the same circumference as the base of the silver bowl. Below these elements are two tiers of long wood bases which are full of small shields for winners' names. On either side of the top of the base are two hockey players.

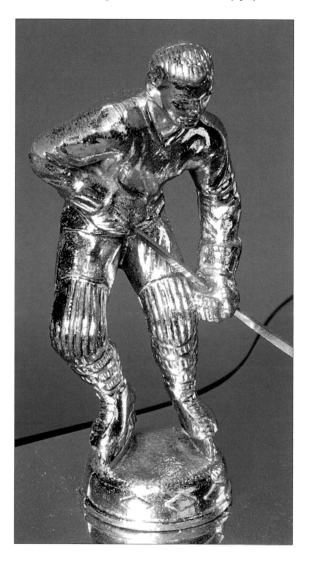

GENESIS

John Ross Robertson, president of the OHA from 1901 to 1905, gave the Memorial Cup to the Ontario Hockey Association in 1919 as an award for the national amateur champions of Canada. In 1921, the CAHA formally took control of the trophy. In 1933, it was awarded to the champion Junior A team in the country, and beginning in 1970 to the top Major Junior team. This distinction was made by the CAHA to separate the top three junior leagues (now called OHL, QMJHL, and WHL) from the provincial junior leagues which would now compete for the Centennial Cup.

FIRST WINNER

The University of Toronto Schools were the top team in the OHA in 1918-19 and faced a challenge from the Regina Patricias, champions of Western Canada (Abbott Cup winners). In a two-game, total goals series, UTS clobbered the Patricias 14-3 and 15-5 at Mutual Street Arena in Toronto. The most famous members of that team included Dunc Munro, who had a fine NHL career, and Joe Sullivan, who later played for Canada at the Olympics and was named to the Senate after his playing days.

CHAMPIONS' HISTORY

Like the Allan Cup, there was an era in hockey when the Memorial Cup was on almost equal footing with the Stanley Cup. In large part this was due to the utterly consuming east-west rivalry, born of geographic competition. Too, the rivalries took shape because the top junior teams were owned by NHL teams and as such represented junior versions of great NHL rivalries. St. Mike's and the Marlboros, for instance, both in Toronto and both sponsored by the Leafs, presented many classic battles for the Memorial Cup, and Toronto and Winnipeg staged many a barn-burning best-of-seven series that rivaled most Stanley Cup finals. Virtually every great NHL star began his career in junior hockey in Canada, though the last 20 years or so has seen a slight shift as some Canadians opt to play in colleges in the United States and go through NCAA hockey to the pros. Although the Toronto Marlboros have been inactive for more than two decades, they still have won more Memorial Cups (seven) than any other team. St. Mike's and Oshawa Generals have both won four times. The most recent dynasty is Kamloops, the Blazers winning three times in four years (1992, 1994, 1995). The current round-robin format to determine a Memorial Cup winner began in 1972, a year after the trophy became exclusive to major junior hockey. Three teams (champions of the OHL, QMJHL, and WHL) met to determine a winner, and later a fourth team, representing the host city, was also included in the format.

TODAY

By 2002, the original Memorial Cup was determined to be too fragile for the wear and tear of travel and winners' pandemonium and was donated by the CHL to the Hockey Hall of Fame. At the same time, a new Memorial Cup was crafted that was virtually identical and would continue to be awarded yearly to the top junior team in Canada. In 2004-05, it was the London Knights that won, defeating Rimouski in a classic showdown featuring London's Corey Perry and the Oceanic's Sidney Crosby.

(left) Detail of one of the silver players that stand posed atop the base of the trophy; (above) shields with winning rosters as they appear on the side of the base.

Symbolic of major junior hockey supremacy in Canada, the Memorial Cup is arguably the most difficult trophy to win because more than 50 teams in three leagues (WHL, OHL, QMJHL) vie for it every year. Teams must, therefore, first win a series of playoff games within their league, and then win a final round played against the other league champions.

TROPHY TO WILLIAM HEWITT

1920

THE NAME

William Hewitt, the father of the more famous Foster, was secretary of the OHA and was the most important member of the Canadian party that traveled to Antwerp, Belgium for the 1920 Olympic Games.

THE TROPHY

Only 11" tall, this commemorative 'thank you' from the players to the team leader weighs only about one pound. The wood base supports an elongated cup with simple heart-shaped handles, and the inscription consists of two parts, on either side. The first reads: "13/To Mr. and Mrs. W.A. Hewitt from the Falcon Hockey Club of Winnipeg/Worlds Amateur Ice Hockey Champions 1920." On the other side: "In appreciation of kindness shown us while representing Canada at the 7th Olympiade Belgium 1920."

GENESIS

The first time hockey was played at the Olympics came in 1920 at the Summer games in Antwerp, Belgium. The Summer Games were held in September of that year while the Winter portion took place in April. Canada sent the Winnipeg Falcons, Allan Cup winners just weeks earlier, to represent that country in the inaugural event. William Hewitt led the team to the tournament and so impressed officials in Antwerp by his knowledge of the sport that they asked him to referee the first game, Sweden versus Belgium. He displayed such a fine interpretation of hockey that the IOC adopted CAHA rules as the official Olympic rules. Hewitt, in fact, was secretary of the OHA from 1903 to 1961 and manager of the CAHA from 1928 to '61. In 1914, he and Claude Robinson created the CAHA. Hewitt later was manager of the 1924 and 1928 Canadian Olympics teams as well. It was his idea to add fishnets to the posts of a net to more easily determine if a puck crossed the goal line or not. In 1925, he and son, Foster, called the first ever horse race by radio, the King's Plate. He was also sports editor of the Toronto Star from 1900 to 1931, a post he quit to become attractions manager at the newly-built Maple Leaf Gardens, where his son would soon take up near permanent residence.

Detail from the inscription on the trophy to William Hewitt for his successful leadership at the 1920 Olympics.

The first Olympic Winter Games took place in 1924, but the modern Summer Olympics started in 1896, making 1920 the 7th Olympiade at which hockey made its debut. Canada, led by team manager, secretary, and referee William Hewitt, easily won gold.

ORIGINAL WORLD CHAMPIONSHIP TROPHY

1920–1939

THE NAME

The World Championships have been in annual competition since 1930 (excluding Olympics years until 1992) and are emblematic of international supremacy.

THE TROPHY

Simple but spectacular, this trophy was never given to any one team for victory at the World Championship. Instead, the names of the winning teams from 1928 to 1939 are engraved in one bronze plaque along the side of the back of the base. The bronze figure is, simply, of hockey player Willy Krietz whose name is scratched into the base of the sculpture.

GENESIS

Ever since 1920, when hockey was first played at the Olympics, it was clear that the sport was popular enough to support an annual tournament, although it was another decade before this opinion gained enough support in Europe for the idea to see the light of day. In the 1920s, only the three Olympics (1920, '24, '28) saw true international competition in hockey.

FIRST WINNER

Up until the Soviet Union entered IIHF competition in 1954, Canada ruled the ice lanes with impunity, recording an almost perfect record for some 34 years.

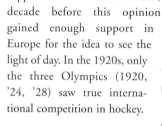

From 1930, when the World Championships became annual, to 1939, when play ceased because of World War II, Canada lost only once, at the 1936 Olympics to a team from Great Britain made up primarily of Canadian-born players. In 1930, for instance, Canada was given a bye directly to the gold medal game, an unfathomable compliment today! The team defeated Germany 6-1 to win the first World Championship (Canada had won gold at the Olympics in 1920, 1924, and 1928). In 1931, Canada did not allow a single goal against in five games and won gold again. In 1932, Canada won gold at the Olympics again, but the next year the team lost 2-1 to the U.S. in the final game, its first international loss ever. The next year, Canada exacted revenge by defeating the Americans by the same 2-1 score for the gold, and in 1935 the Canadians beat Switzerland 4-2 for gold. The 1936 loss was the country's only Olympics blemish to date, but from 1937 to 1939, Canada had a record of 23-0-1 and outscored its opponents 119-11. After the final victory in 1939, the IIHF gave the championship trophy to the Canadians in recognition of their vast superiority. During these years, the CAHA usually sent the Allan Cup winners overseas to represent Canada at the World Championships and Olympics, even though the competition was fielding the best players in their country. The IIHF regarded amateur play with the strictest attitude, and it wasn't until 1977 that Canada sent professionals to the Worlds. The 1938 team came from the Trail Smoke Eaters and had a perfect 8-0 record. The team outscored its opponents 42-1 as goalie Duke Scodellaro was beaten only once, by Czechoslovakia. In the final series of round-robin games Canada beat Switzerland 7-0, Czechoslovakia 4-0, and USA also 4-0 to win gold.

CHAMPIONS' HISTORY

There have been a number of World Championship trophies over the years, but the top nations have remained consistently so from decade to decade. Canada's run of victories ended by the 1960s when the Soviets were sending their top pro-trained players to play Canada's university students, and it wasn't until 1994 that Canada won gold for the first time since the Trail Smoke Eaters in 1961. In that same span, the Soviets won 21 titles.

TODAY

Canada's renaissance as world leaders is reflected in success at the World Championships. The country won both the 2003 and 2004 tournaments to go along with Olympic gold for the men and women (2002), World Cup of Hockey championship in 2004, World Championships gold for the women, and gold for the World Juniors in 2005. No country has ever held as many titles at one time as Canada in early 2005. These remarkable bragging rights ended a short time later as the Canadian national women's team lost the World Championship gold medal game to USA 1-0 in a shootout and the men lost 3-0 to the Czech Republic in the gold medal game at the 2005 World Championship in Austria.

(left) Side view of the trophy; (above) two panels from the side of the wood base include the pertinent information to the trophy's purpose.

In the European tradition, this is really a sculpture created specifically as a prize for hockey (as opposed to the Canadian way of creating a trophy for annual competition). Further to the European way, this World Championship trophy was not in circulation year after year.

HART TROPHY

1923-PRESENT

THE NAME

The Hart Trophy is named after Cecil Hart, manager and coach of the Montreal Canadiens.

THE TROPHY

The original Hart Trophy consists of a square, wood base supporting a long, unadorned silver trophy on top. Each side of the square base accommodates nine plaques with the names of the winning players. The inscription adheres to an early tradition of awards whereby any player who achieves a "hat trick" of wins can claim ownership of the trophy: "Presented by Dr. David Hart of Montreal to the National Hockey League for its most valuable player/To be won three times before becoming the property of any one player."

GENESIS

The trophy was donated to the NHL in 1923 by Dr. David Hart, father of Cecil, and it is the oldest trophy in the NHL showcase. In fact, it was Hart's naming of the trophy that began the uniquely hockey trend of honouring a great man of the sport with an eponymous trophy. Dr. Hart led a remarkable life. He was a Jewish physician in Montreal and the first president of that city's Zionist Society. During the Fenian Raids (1866-70), he was a captain in the Prince of Wales Fusiliers. He was also a prominent Mason. What few fans today know is that he intended the trophy to honour the league's most "useful" player, but the term quickly came to be interpreted as "most valuable player." His son, Cecil, was active in the amateur sporting scene in Montreal starting in 1900, primarily in baseball and hockey. In 1921, Cecil helped orchestrate the sale of the Montreal Canadiens, and for his efforts he was named a director to the team. In 1924, he briefly assumed the general manager's position for the cross-town, English rivals, the Maroons, but conflicts within the organization led to his early departure. Cecil coached the Canadiens from 1926 to 1932, winning two Stanley Cup championships in the springs of '30 and '31, before retiring. When the Habs fell on hard times, he was persuaded to return, in 1936, and took the team to a first place finish in his first year back. Hart was forced to retire during his third season because of illness, and he died in the summer of 1940. In 1960, with the wood base of the original trophy full, the NHL retired the trophy to the Hockey Hall of Fame and created a radically different award that became known as the Hart Memorial Trophy (see Gallery, page 151).

FIRST WINNER

The first winner of the Hart Trophy was Frank Nighbor of the Ottawa Senators in 1923-24, who won by a single vote over Sprague Cleghorn of the Canadiens, to this day the closest race ever. In 1990, Mark Messier beat Ray Bourque by

two votes. Nighbor's victory also speaks to the original intent of the trophy. He scored just eleven goals and was not among the league's leading scorers; instead, he won on the strength of his overall play.

CHAMPIONS' HISTORY

Of all the league's trophies, the Hart is the most prescient for determining a Hall of Fame player. Only two retired players have won the Hart and are not in the Hockey Hall of Fame. In 1942, Tom Anderson of the Brooklyn Americans won, yet the top scorer, Bryan Hextall, didn't even rank on the final list! In 1954, goalie Al Rollins of Chicago led the league in most losses and most goals allowed, yet he out-voted Red Kelly and Maurice Richard for that year's Hart! Wayne Gretzky won the award nine times, including eight in a row (1979-87) and Gordie Howe, his idol, six times. Furthermore, the Hart is very much a trophy for forwards. Only five goalies have ever won, and only Dominik Hasek has won twice (1996-98; the other four are Roy Worters, Chuck Rayner, Al Rollins, and Jacques Plante).

TODAY

In more recent years, the trophy has become much more closely associated with the Art Ross Trophy, voters feeling the NHL's top scorer is also his team's most valuable player. Since 1961, the two trophies have been awarded to the same player in the same year 21 times. In its first 37 years, this happened just eleven times.

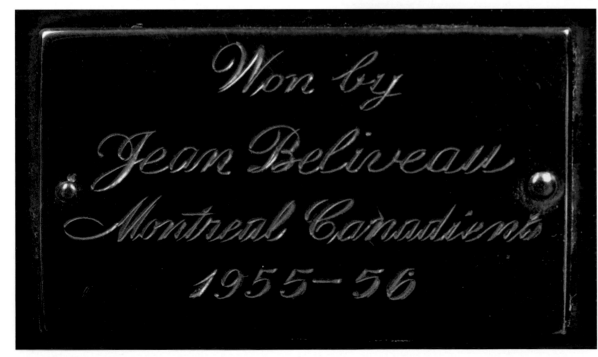

(left) Plaque to recognize Jean Beliveau as Hart Trophy winner; (above) sampling of plaques from the base of the trophy.

The original Hart Trophy bears little resemblance to the current version, but its significance has been consistent for more than 80 years—to honour the league's most valuable player for each NHL season.

PRINCE OF WALES TROPHY

1924-PRESENT

THE NAME

His Royal Highness, the Prince of Wales, donated a trophy in his name to the NHL in 1924.

THE TROPHY

An elaborate combination of numerous design elements, the Prince of Wales Trophy has as its focus perhaps the largest silver bowl of any trophy at the Hockey Hall of Fame. It is more than a foot high, converging toward its bottom, and is supported by four silver hockey sticks the blades of which are soldered into small mounts on a wood base. The top of the base also features four small gold pucks, and in the centre, directly under the bowl, sits an uncut mountain of glass. The base is square, but the four corners have been cut off to produce four small panels upon which winners' names are attached by small silver plaques. These plaques also adorn three of the four larger sides of the base, the fourth holding a plaque bearing the trophy's name.

GENESIS

At the time this trophy was introduced, the NHL's post season consisted of playoff games to determine a league champion. That team then played champions from the west to decide the Stanley Cup winner. Thus, for the first two years, the Prince of Wales Trophy was not awarded to the first place team at the end of the regular season but rather to the NHL champions. In 1926, the NHL became a two-division league and the Prince of Wales was awarded to the league champions. In 1928-29, it finally became a trophy simply for the team finishing first in the American Division (the Canadian Division winners receiving the O'Brien Trophy), and in 1938, when the league again reverted to a one-division

league, the trophy was awarded to the top-place team. In 1967, when the league doubled in size from six teams to twelve, the Prince of Wales was awarded to the first-place team in the East Division to complement the Campbell Bowl which went to the top club in the West. In 1974, the league introduced two conferences within which were two divisions each, and the Prince of Wales Trophy went to the regular season champ of the Wales Conference. Starting in 1981, the trophy was presented to the playoff champion of the conference, and in 1993, when the NHL changed the names of conferences and divisions, it was awarded to the winning playoff team of the Eastern Conference.

FIRST WINNER

The Montreal Canadiens finished second of four teams at the end of the 24-game NHL regular season for 1923-24 and met Ottawa in the NHL playoffs to determine which team would face the Vancouver Millionaires, champions of the west, for the right to play the Calgary Tigers for the Stanley Cup. The Habs won both games of the two-game, total-goals series, 1-0, and 4-2. Against Vancouver, they prevailed by 3-2 and 2-1 scores and then met the Tigers and again came out on top. Montreal won 6-1 and 3-0 to make their playoff record a perfect 6-0 for 1924. Their prize was the Prince of Wales Trophy (as NHL champions) and Stanley Cup (as champions of Canada).

CHAMPIONS' HISTORY

Montreal has won the Prince of Wales Trophy some 24 times, but Detroit and Boston have been well represented over the years as well, notably during the early years of the award. The Canadiens won it the first year (1924) and then not again until 1944 during which time the Bruins won it ten times. The Red Wings had an unprecedented run in the 1950s, winning seven successive years, 1948-55. Since 1984, there has been no one dominant team. Philadelphia, Montreal, and New Jersey have all been Cup finalists three times in the

last two decades, but no team has won the Prince of Wales even three years running since the dynastic Islanders (1982-84) at a time when the awarding of the trophy underwent its transformation from regular-season champs to Cup finalists.

TODAY

The Tampa Bay Lightning, perhaps the most unsung team to win the Stanley Cup in the last half century or longer, won the Prince of Wales en route to their improbable Cup run. Led by captain Dave Andreychuk, the Lightning beat the Islanders in five decisive games in the opening round of the 2004 playoffs, then cruised past Montreal in four straight games. In the conference finals they beat the Flyers 2-1 in game seven to win the Wales Trophy and then beat Calgary in seven to win the Cup.

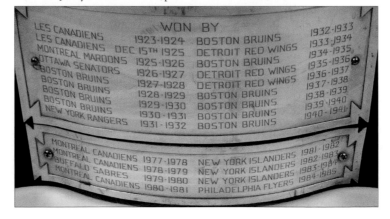

WON BY			
LES CANADIENS	1923-1924	BOSTON BRUINS	1932-1933
LES CANADIENS DEC 15TH	1925	DETROIT RED WINGS	1933-1934
MONTREAL MAROONS	1925-1926	BOSTON BRUINS	1934-1935
OTTAWA SENATORS	1926-1927	DETROIT RED WINGS	1935-1936
BOSTON BRUINS	1927-1928	DETROIT RED WINGS	1936-1937
BOSTON BRUINS	1928-1929	BOSTON BRUINS	1937-1938
BOSTON BRUINS	1929-1930	BOSTON BRUINS	1938-1939
BOSTON BRUINS	1930-1931	BOSTON BRUINS	1939-1940
NEW YORK RANGERS	1931-1932	BOSTON BRUINS	1940-1941

MONTREAL CANADIENS	1977-1978	NEW YORK ISLANDERS	1981-1982
MONTREAL CANADIENS	1978-1979	NEW YORK ISLANDERS	1982-1983
BUFFALO SABRES	1979-1980	NEW YORK ISLANDERS	1983-1984
MONTREAL CANADIENS	1980-1981	PHILADELPHIA FLYERS	1984-1985

(top left) The Art Nouveau name plaque; (above) the coat of arms of the Prince of Wales as it appears near the top of the trophy; (left) a section of winners from the side of the base.

Despite the many changes to the NHL's structure since 1924 when the trophy was introduced, the Prince of Wales has survived and maintained its place among the league's most important honours, currently being given to the champions of the Eastern Conference.

LADY BYNG TROPHY

1924-PRESENT

THE NAME

Lady Byng was wife of Lord Byng of Vimy, Canada's Governor General from 1921 to 1926.

THE TROPHY

The current and newer version of the trophy features a large, square base, one with a large silver plaque which lists the names of previous winners, the other three sides with small, individual plaques for each winner. The largest plaque lists winners from 1924-25 (Frank Nighbor, Ottawa) through to 1949-50 (Edgar Laprade, Rangers). Each of the three other sides hold 20 plaques each and will be filled with the winner for 2010-11. The inscription on the silver vase above is explanatory: "Viscountess Byng of Vimy Memorial Trophy/Replacing the Viscountess Byng of Vimy Challenge Cup presented to the National Hockey League 1935/To encourage clean sportsmanship."

GENESIS

Lady and Lord Byng were hockey fans of the first order and attended many NHL games, notably in Ottawa during their

residence at Rideau Hall. They admired the speed and skill of the game and particularly were fans of Frank Nighbor, a skilled, scoring forward who was also a sporting and gentlemanly player. In admiration of his skills, Lady Byng presented him a trophy at the conclusion of the 1924-25 season, a trophy he won the next year as well. After Lady Byng's death in 1949, the NHL presented a new trophy in her honour called the Lady Byng Memorial Trophy.

FIRST WINNER

Although Nighbor won the first two Byng Trophies, sporting play and skill were the trademarks of Frank Boucher of the Rangers. He won his first Byng Trophy in 1928 (Billy Burch of the New York Americans won it in the third year), the first of seven times over the next eight years that he was so honoured. So enamored was Lady Byng of Boucher's play that after that seventh winning, in 1935, she gave him the trophy and crafted a new one for the NHL to donate in perpetuity.

CHAMPIONS' HISTORY

No player has equaled Boucher's seven victories of this trophy, but it is often given to a player noted for his offense who accrues few penalty minutes during a season. In many years it is almost considered a runner-up trophy to the Hart Trophy. Oddly, only two defencemen have ever won the award, both Red Wings: Red Kelly, three times in four years

in the first half of the 1950s, and Bill Quackenbush in 1948-49. Wayne Gretzky won the Byng five times and the aforementioned Kelly four times (once as a forward, with Toronto, in 1960-61). The most amazing winner was surely Stan Mikita who won consecutive Byng's in '66-'67 and '67-'68. Why amazing? Because in four of his first six full seasons in the NHL he had more than 100 penalty minutes! But Chicago coach Billy Reay convinced him that he would become a better player if he focused on playing his game and staying out of the penalty box (i.e., avoid fighting). In his two Byng years, Mikita also won the Hart Trophy as the league's leading scorer, proof positive of Reay's theory.

TODAY

Although the trophy continues to be a "forwards only" award, Detroit defenceman Nicklas Lidstrom has been a runner-up four times since 1999, giving hope that one day a blueliner will again be honoured for his combined skills of playing ability and sportsmanship. In the evermore macho NHL, however, there appears to be a greater stigma attached to the trophy, no one in the world of hockey wanting to win a trophy that is dedicated to clean and fair play!

(left) One side of the base consisting of individual plaques for annual winners; (top) detail of the inscription on the bowl of the trophy; (above) two more inscriptions honouring the most gentlemanly player.

Like many trophies, the Lady Byng consists of a beautiful example of silverware to which is attached a base which can hold winners' names for many decades, all the time maintaining a consistent appearance and glamour.

GEORGES VEZINA TROPHY

1926-PRESENT

THE NAME

Georges Vezina was the first superstar goalie in hockey, a man who for 15 years played every game consecutively for the Montreal Canadiens (1910-1925). Tragically, his Iron Man streak ended when he had to leave a game on November 28, 1925, because of serious illness, and he died of tuberculosis just a few months later.

THE TROPHY

Given to the NHL by the Montreal Canadiens in honour of their great goalie who had recently passed away, the Georges Vezina Trophy is as funerary as it gets. The mausoleum-style tribute features four pillars within which is held a goal net to identify Vezina's position. Crossed goalie sticks held by a commemorative wreath sit under one side of the pillars. Above the roof rests a puck, and, oddly, on top of this a beaver is perched. The wood base consists of two huge sections. On one side of the upper tier is a photo of Vezina and to either side are attached long silver plaques honouring the first two winners, appropriately George Hainsworth, Vezina's successor in the Canadiens' goal. Between the two tiers is a flat shoulder which can also accommodate more names, and today the trophy is now full. As a result, the Hockey Hall of Fame has added a new base which will accomodate names for many years to come.

GENESIS

The tragic death of Vezina—hockey star one minute, tuberculosis patient the next—inspired Montreal's three owners to donate a trophy to the NHL to honour the goalie who allowed the fewest goals each season. Joe Cattarinich, Louis Letourneau, and Leo Dandurand made the donation for the 1926-27 season, the first year after Vezina succumbed to his illness.

FIRST WINNER

Fittingly it was George Hainsworth, the man who replaced Vezina on a full-time basis in the Canadiens' net, who won the first Vezina. In 1926-27, he played all 44 of the Canadiens' games and led the league with 14 shutouts along the way. He allowed just 67 goals all year. Hainsworth also won the second Vezina and the third as well, and by the time he retired in 1937 he had accrued a hall of fame's worth of greatness to go with his three trophies and two Stanley Cup wins with the Canadiens (in 1930 and '31).

CHAMPIONS' HISTORY

Vezina Trophy winners represent a veritable who's who of hall of fame goalies. In Original Six days, the dominant figures included Montreal goalie Bill Durnan, the last goalie captain, who won the trophy six times in seven years in the 1940s. Terry Sawchuk won it three times in the early 1950s and then Jacques Plante led the league five years in a row at the same time as his Canadiens were winning five Cups in a row (1955-60). Beginning with the 1964-65 season, the NHL mandated that all teams had to dress two goalies. As a result, the Vezina became a shared trophy between the team's starter and his reliable backup. From 1964 until 1982, when the Vezina became an MVP-style voted trophy, only three goalies won the Vezina on their own: Tony Esposito in 1969-70, Ken Dryden in 1972-73 and '75-'76, and Bernie Parent in '74-'75. The only tie in trophy history came in the '73-'74

season when both Chicago and Philadelphia allowed just 164 goals over the course of the season. Although Parent's GAA was lower than Esposito's (1.89 vs. 2.03), the goalie was really representative of the team and the two split the honours. Similarly, in 1950-51, Toronto allowed just 138 goals and Detroit 139. Al Rollins played most of the games for the Leafs and won the Vezina because of the team goals allowed, even though Terry Sawchuk played all 70 games for the Red Wings and had a lower average than Rollins! With the exception of that tie in '73-'74, the Vezina has been shared by future hall of famers only twice. In 1966-67, Sawchuk and Johnny Bower led the league in GAA and took the Leafs to the Cup. In '68-'69, St. Louis coach Scotty Bowman utilized Plante and Glenn Hall in an aged but remarkable tandem that also surrendered the fewest goals in the league.

TODAY

Since 1981-82, with the introduction of the Jennings Trophy, the Vezina has been awarded by vote of the league's general managers to determine the best goalie based on play, not goals-against average. Dominik Hasek has won the new Vezina a staggering six times in eight years (1993-2001), Patrick Roy three times, and Martin Brodeur twice, including 2003-04.

(left) A small, silver goal net rests ominously within the crypt-like setting of the trophy; (middle) Vezina's name engraved on the side of the trophy; (above) a small portrait of Vezina from the side of the wood base.

Because the base of the Georges Vezina Trophy is now full, the Hockey Hall of Fame has added a new one to ensure many more names can be added to the original trophy for years to come.

ATLANTIC CITY BOARDWALK TROPHY

1931-1973

THE NAME

In 1931, the Convention Hall of Atlantic City (an arena) commissioned a trophy to be awarded to the annual national AAU champions (Amateur Athletic Union). The next year, the league became the Eastern Amateur Hockey League (EAHL).

THE TROPHY

It is as original as it is unknown, as beautiful as it is long, long forgotten. The Boardwalk Challenge Trophy is entirely gold with a black wood base, the latter of which is only about six inches high and as wide as the gold base of the trophy. The middle section is a single, thick column with the name of the trophy on one third of the circumference and a hockey scene etched above it. A second third provides all the details for the first winners, the 1931-32 Atlantic City Sea Gulls, and the last third lists winners from the Eastern Amateur Hockey League series from 1937-38 to 1948-49. Above this are perched three eagles with wings spread holding a globe which rests underneath a model of Nike, the goddess of Victory. Because the gold trophy itself is full, the base was added to accommodate shield-shaped plaques with winners later than what are engraved on the trophy, nine in all.

GENESIS

Tommy Lockhart was the president of the Amateur Hockey Association of the United States as well as the EAHL, and it

was through his efforts to establish an annual trophy to legitimize the game and league in the U.S. that led to the continuance of the Boardwalk Trophy.

FIRST WINNER

Fittingly, it was the local Atlantic City Sea Gulls that won the first championship, in 1931-32. Ray Levia and Herb Foster, both natives of Brockville, Ontario, were on that team as were lesser lights such as goalie Benny Haynes, defenders Jack Housley and Val Proulx, and forwards Jack McKinnon and Ted Hunter.

CHAMPIONS' HISTORY

The Sea Gulls won the league championship again two years later but then the Boardwalk Trophy was mothballed for four years until Lockhart convinced the governing body to allow the EAHL to claim the trophy for its champions. It remained in circulation until 1973 (by which time the league was known simply at the EHL, the "amateur" in the title long giving way to professionalism) when the league folded, a victim to the WHA which was gobbling up U.S. hockey cities as fast as it could. That was also the year Lockhart retired, so the trophy's and league's strongest advocate was no longer active to champion the trophy's cause. The Johnstown Jets, known more famously years later for their brawling in the movie *Slapshot*, won the trophy five times in the decade 1952-62. Ironically, at some time in the early 1970s, the EHL actually awarded the Walker Cup to the league champions but continued to hand out the Boardwalk Trophy to the team captain after the final game! Other winners through the years include the Long Island Ducks, Boston Olympics, and Clinton Comets.

TODAY

Brian Elwell was captain of the Syracuse Blazers, last winners of the Boardwalk Trophy, in 1972-73. He settled in Syracuse after retiring and opened a restaurant. One day in 1987, he received an anonymous phone call asking if he'd like to have the trophy that had long disappeared for the hockey consciousness of the area. Elwell said yes, stored it, and then promptly forgot all about it until about seven years later when he decided to re-locate his restaurant. He contacted Chuck Miller, a history buff by day and a local hockey writer for the AHL's Albany River Rats by night. Miller did endless research on the league and trophy, discovering its provenance and importance to the EAHL through the years, and eventually convincing Elwell to give it to him. They agreed that the trophy, battered yet beautiful and an important part of hockey history, belonged in the Hockey Hall of Fame, and it was duly sent to the Hall in Toronto by Miller.

(left) Shields holding the names of winners; (above) detail of the front section of the trophy depicting a hockey scene and accompanied by the trophy's name and purpose.

Not every winning team's name appears on the base of the trophy, but the Atlantic City Boardwalk Trophy nonetheless was around for more than forty years in various minor pro leagues, its purpose malleable, its attractiveness undeniable.

GEORGE RICHARDSON MEMORIAL TROPHY

1931-1980

THE NAME

A noted hockey player from Kingston, Lieutenant George Richardson died overseas on February 9, 1916, during action in World War I. In April 1932, his brother, James, donated a trophy in George's name to be presented annually to the champion junior team of Eastern Canada (Ontario, Quebec, The Maritimes).

THE TROPHY

The Richardson trophy in many ways conforms to the classic model of what a hockey trophy looks like. The sterling silver bowl sits on a black wood base, in this case square. The bowl's name is inscribed in large block letters on the outside lip, and the side has further description of what the award represents. The square base has three sides with small plaques with winners' names, and to the fourth is affixed a large rectangle of silver magnificently depicting a typical hockey scene.

GENESIS

In the early days of junior hockey, a team from the East played a team from the West in the Memorial Cup finals. As a result, the champion of the Ontario league played the best from Quebec and The Maritimes to decide the Eastern repre-

sentative in the Memorial Cup. This winner received the Richardson Trophy. However, the 1971 Memorial Cup went to a new format in which three teams played a round robin series, those three being the winners of the Ontario league, Quebec league, and Western league. As a result, there was no further playoff between Ontario, Quebec, and The Maritimes and the Richardson Trophy was retired.

FIRST WINNER

The Sudbury Wolves won the first edition of the Richardson Trophy in 1931-32 and carried on to defeat the Winnipeg Monarchs and claim the Memorial Cup. Coach Sam Rothschild's team beat the Montreal AAA in the East to qualify for the national junior championship. The team was led by the great Toe Blake and also featured Dalton Smith and goalie Anthony Healey. The finals were held at Shea's Amphitheatre in Winnipeg, and the Wolves won the best-of-three with a dramatic 1-0 win in the deciding game. Smith scored the only goal of the game, and Healey was outstanding in goal.

CHAMPIONS' HISTORY

Teams from the East (i.e., Richardson Trophy winners) invariably went on to win the Memorial Cup. The Oshawa Generals won the Richardson Trophy three successive years (1937-40), winning the Memorial Cup as well the last two times. Those teams included future NHLers Billy Taylor, Frank Eddolls, the McAtee brothers—Norm and Jud—and

Nick Knott. After a year's absence, the Gens won another three Richardson championships in a row, one of those turning into another more cherished Memorial Cup championship as well (1944). The St. Mike's Majors also won three in a row (1944-47) under coach Joe Primeau, featuring a who's who of future NHL stars: Red Kelly, Jim Morrison, Ed Sandford, Benny Woit, Rudy Migay, and Gus Mortson. No team has ever won three successive Memorial Cup tournaments. The Toronto Marlboros have an amazing record: they won the Richardson Trophy four times between 1955 and 1967, and each time they went on to win the Memorial Cup. The back-to-back Marlies of 1955 and '56 had in their lineup Bobby Baun, Bob Pulford, and Bob Nevin and were coached by the legendary Leafs goalie of a generation earlier, Turk Broda. The Montreal Junior Canadiens were the last mini-dynasty for these two trophies. They won consecutively in 1969 and 1970 on what were arguably the greatest junior teams ever. The roster included Gilbert Perreault, Rick Martin, Marc Tardif, Ian Turnbull, Jocelyn Guevremont, J-P Bordeleau, and Jim Rutherford. The Richardson Trophy may honour junior players in Eastern Canada, but the truth is it prophesied great players of the NHL as well.

TODAY

Each of the three major junior leagues in Canada has a regular season champions trophy and a playoff champion trophy, but after that those teams, plus the host city, all gather for the Memorial Cup tournament which features each of the four teams playing a round robin, the top two in the standings advancing to a Memorial Cup-deciding contest. The Richardson Trophy served its purpose for three decades, but it is no longer in circulation.

(left) A hockey scene on the front of the base; (above) detail of the lip and rim of the bowl.

It might not be the most easily identifiable trophy in the Hockey Hall of Fame's collection, but the Richardson Trophy was won by many future great stars of the NHL and was in its own right a special championship award for excellence at the highest level of amateur hockey in Canada.

CALDER CUP

THE NAME

Frank Calder was the first president of the NHL, from the league's inception in 1917 to his sudden death in 1943. During that time, he was instrumental in placing NHL teams in what later became Original Six hockey cities in the U.S. (Boston, Chicago, Detroit, New York), and he also helped establish the AHL as an affiliate organization to the NHL.

THE TROPHY

The Calder Cup is defined by two distinct parts, the original, as it were, and the makeshift extension. The silver bowl is a beautiful creation only about a foot high with two side handles. The rim features ornate silverwork, and there are several engravings on the bowl for some of the early champions. The 1938 Providence Reds, for instance, are identified near the bottom of the Cup, but only the president, manager, and coach are mentioned by name. The 1939, 1940, and 1941 champions are similarly listed, but then the square wood base holds all champions' names in a simple list. In fact, only the first name is given (i.e., "1957 Cleveland").

GENESIS

In the fall of 1936, the International Hockey League and the Can-Am League amalgamated to form the IAHL (International-American Hockey League). The new league decided to inaugurate a new trophy to its champions, dedicating it to Frank Calder.

FIRST WINNER

The Syracuse Stars finished first overall in the Western Division of the IAHL and went on to win the first Calder Cup. As would be the case so often in the future, virtually every player from this team later played in the NHL, Murray Armstrong, George Parsons, Normie Mann, and Phil Stein among that number with the Stars. Ironically, it was the first and only time Syracuse won the trophy.

CHAMPIONS' HISTORY

The Cleveland Barons (defunct) won the Calder Cup nine times during their existence (1936-72) and the still-active Hershey Bears have won eight times. In 1971, the Nova

Scotia Voyageurs, an affiliate of the Montreal Canadiens, became the first Canadian team to win. In all, more than 100 players have won both the Calder Cup and Stanley Cup, and some 18 of that number have gone on to be inducted into the Hockey Hall of Fame, notably Terry Sawchuk, Johnny Bower, Al Arbour, and Gerry Cheevers. The Springfield Indians, under the mercurial guidance of Eddie Shore, are the only team to win three Calder Cups in succession, a feat they performed from 1959 to 1962. The connection between an AHL team's success and its parent club is irrefutable, as the success of the former often leads to the success of the latter. When the Voyageurs won in 1972, the Canadiens won the Stanley Cup the following year. The Voyageurs won again in 1976 and '77 as the Habs were winning Cups annually. The Albany River Rats won the Calder in 1994-95 and the same year their parent club, New Jersey, won its first Cup. The Saint John Flames won in 2000-01, and three years later the team went to game seven of the Stanley Cup finals.

TODAY

The AHL remains the prime resource for NHL development and talent. It now boasts 27 teams for 2005-06, virtually all with NHL affiliation, and when NHL clubs speak of "the farm" they generally mean the AHL. The 2004-05 Calder Cup winners were the Philadelphia Phantoms as they swept Chicago with a 5-2 win in game four before an AHL record crowd of 20,103 at the Wachovia Center in Philadelphia, home to the parent club Flyers. The Phantoms were a team loaded with players with NHL experience, from MVP goalie Antero Niittymaki to Patrick Sharp, Jon Sim, Todd Fedoruk, John Slaney, and Joni Pitkanen.

(above) Providence is one of the few teams whose name appears right on the bowl itself; (below) the front panel with winning teams' names.

AWARDED TO THE
CHAMPIONS OF THE AMERICAN HOCKEY LEAGUE

1937 SYRACUSE	1947 HERSHEY	1957 CLEVELAND
1938 PROVIDENCE	1948 CLEVELAND	1958 HERSHEY
1939 CLEVELAND	1949 PROVIDENCE	1959 HERSHEY
1940 PROVIDENCE	1950 INDIANAPOLIS	1960 SPRINGFIELD
1941 CLEVELAND	1951 CLEVELAND	1961 SPRINGFIELD
1942 INDIANAPOLIS	1952 PITTSBURGH	1962 SPRINGFIELD
1943 BUFFALO	1953 CLEVELAND	1963 BUFFALO
1944 BUFFALO	1954 CLEVELAND	1964 CLEVELAND
1945 CLEVELAND	1955 PITTSBURGH	1965 ROCHESTER
1946 BUFFALO	1956 PROVIDENCE	1966 ROCHESTER

The most important minor professional trophy in North America, the Calder Cup continues to be awarded annually to the champions of the American Hockey League, the 2004-05 winners being the Philadelphia Phantoms.

CALDER TROPHY

1936-PRESENT

THE NAME

Frank Calder was the NHL president from 1917 to his untimely death in 1943, a driving force behind the creation of the NHL.

THE TROPHY

Like many of the older trophies still in circulation, the Calder is an original trophy that now rests on a wood base to allow all winners' names to be displayed with the trophy. In the case of the Calder, the original six winners were engraved right on the silver trophy, but thereafter names were engraved on small silver plaques that were mounted onto the side of the wood base. Each side of each of the two bases holds 12 names, the top tier of the base now full and the lower now half filled itself. Interestingly, there are also four winners of the Calder listed on the trophy who were named rookie of the year prior to the introduction of the award! Winners from 1932-36 share equal billing on the three-handled mug anachronistically.

GENESIS

The first trophy was presented at the conclusion of the 1936-37 season as a way for Calder to make official a practice that had been ongoing for several years by sportswriters to conduct a poll and name the best rookie of each NHL season. Calder made his trophy all the more special because each year until his death he had a new edition minted for the player to keep. After his passing, the NHL created one trophy that would be presented annually as the Calder Memorial Trophy.

FIRST WINNER

Syl Apps of Toronto was the first winner of the NHL's rookie of the year award, and what a fitting beginning to the trophy's history! Apps was a superstar, a gentleman on and off the ice, and a future member of the Hockey Hall of Fame, without question one of the game's greatest stars of the Original Six. Prior to Apps, writers had recently voted Russ Blinco of the Maroons the best rookie of '33-'34, Sweeney Schriner of the New York Americans the next year, and Chicago goalie Mike Karakas the best of '35-'36.

CHAMPIONS' HISTORY

By definition, the Calder is the only trophy a player can win only once in his career, and because it's awarded at the start of a player's career it is, like the Entry Draft, a bit of a crap shoot. Future greats such as Terry Sawchuk, Frank Mahovlich, Gilbert Perreault, and Mario Lemieux have won the Calder, but so have players who went on to have less than stellar careers: John Quilty, Ed Litzenberger, Steve Vickers, Willi Plett. But the trophy is not intended to predict which players will be stars, only to indicate which first year players had the best single, introductory year in the NHL. The Calder also has a more chequered history than most other individual awards because there is always the question as to what constitutes a rookie. Today, the rules stipulate that a player must not have played 25 games in any previous season or six games in any two seasons of a pro league. It further states that a player has to be 26 years of age or younger as of September 15 of his rookie season. The latter rule was instituted by the NHL in 1990 after Sergei Makarov, a 27-year-old veteran of Soviet league hockey, was named winner of the Calder Trophy for 1989-90. It was a rule that tried to deal with the influx of European players who were coming to the NHL later in their careers and who had played at a high level for a decade or more, just not in the NHL. Ironically, though, Tony Esposito would not have won the award in '69-'70, when he was a legitimate rookie, but neither would Peter Stastny in '80-'81 who had played in Czechoslovakia for years and was no more a rookie than Makarov. Perhaps now that the NHL has recruited players the world over the Calder can return to its roots and eliminate the need for an age requirement. The Original Six teams lead the way in Calder victors, Toronto with nine, Boston and the Rangers eight, Chicago and Montreal six, and Detroit four. Since expansion in 1967, the Islanders with four lead the way of the new teams. Amazingly, the last Leafs player to win was Brit Selby in 1966; the last Habs was Ken Dryden in 1972, and the last Red Wings was Roger Crozier in 1965.

TODAY

Time will tell if recent Calder winners are Hall of Famers or one-season wonders, but one thing is for sure: it is the most disparate of awards. In the last ten years, nine teams can boast a Calder winner, only Boston having two top rookies (Sergei Samsonov in '97-'98 and goalie Andrew Raycroft, most recently, in 2003-04).

(left) Detail of the bowl; (below) one small section of winners shows the wide range of talent and the generally consistent ability of the players to have long and successful NHL careers.

A high level of play by players in their first NHL season guarantees nothing for the future, but many a Calder winner has gone on to a career worthy of induction into the Hockey Hall of Fame, from Syl Apps to Terry Sawchuk to, more recently, Mario Lemieux, Ray Bourque, and Peter Stastny.

THOMAS O'CONNELL MEMORIAL TROPHY

1938-1959

THE NAME

Thomas A.S. O'Connell was an alderman in Montreal.

THE TROPHY

Slender and not particularly heavy, the O'Connell trophy has the traditional presentation of two wood bases supporting a trophy on top. The variation on the theme is that the bases are narrow and have one gold band wrapped around each part of the base to accommodate winners' names. The trophy above is simple gold with an inscription demarcating its significance. The top of the lid features a wreath symbolizing victory.

GENESIS

In need of a trophy to honour the league champions prior to the Allan Cup playdowns, the Quebec Senior Hockey League accepted a donation from D'Arcy and Daniel O'Connell in memory of their father for the honour. It was competed for from 1938-39 until the end of the QSHL in 1958-59.

FIRST WINNER

The Montreal Royals of 1938-39 were the first winners of the O'Connell Trophy, their first of three successive league championships. The team was coached by Frank Carlin and featured the "Light Brigade" forward line of Buddy O'Connor, Pete Morin, and Gerry Heffernan, all of whom later played for the Montreal Canadiens. Morin played half of one year, 1941-42, and Heffernan played two full seasons, winning a Cup with the Habs in '43-'44. O'Connor, though, played ten years in the NHL, 1941-51, six of those coming with the Canadiens. The Light Brigade Line racked up 81 points for the Royals in their 22-game schedule and led the team to the Allan Cup finals against the Port Arthur Bearcats. The Bearcats won the best-of-five series three games to one, and all games were played to sold out crowds at the Forum in Montreal. The winner of this series was supposed to represent Canada at the 1940 Olympic Winter Games, but the event was cancelled because of World War II. The QSHL this year featured seven teams: the Royals were the class of the league, Ottawa placed second and Concordia (coached by Sylvio Mantha) placed third. Aurel Joliat's Verdun team finished in fourth followed by the Victorias, McGill. The Quebec Aces, which had won the league championship the previous two seasons, finished dead last.

CHAMPIONS' HISTORY

Only once did the QSHL champions go on to win the Allan Cup. In 1946-47, the Montreal Royals did the trick, the first Montreal team to do so since 1929-30 when AAA won the senior amateur championship of Canada. The '46-'47 Royals were coached again by Frank Carlin and featured future Canadiens' greats Gerry McNeil in goal and Hall of Fame defenceman Doug Harvey. The Royals also won the last O'Connell Trophy, in '58-'59, beating the Trois-Rivieres Lions in the best-of-nine playoffs five games to three. The QSHL was popular, to be sure, but the league thrived in the early 1950s on the strength of their greatest star, Jean Beliveau. He played for the Quebec Aces for two full seasons, 1951-53, and in that first season, at the age of 20, he won the scoring championship by three points over Les Douglas of the Royals. The Aces were league champions in '51-'52, and although they finished in sixth place the next year, Beliveau won the scoring title again (Chicoutimi won the O'Connell Trophy in '52-'53). In '53-'54, Beliveau now a star in the NHL, the Aces finished fourth in the regular season standings but beat all comers in the playoffs to win the O'Connell for the second time in three years, this time after besting the Ottawa Senators in the final game of the best-of-nine series.

TODAY

There is no similar senior pro league in Quebec today. All of the province's best players go quickly to the NHL or are developed or demoted to the AHL or lesser leagues in North America or Europe. As a result, the O'Connell went out of circulation in 1959 and has been a museum piece ever since.

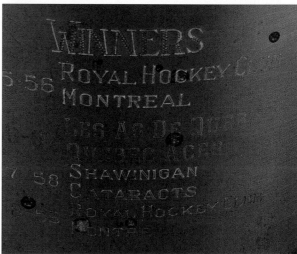

(left) Detail of the commemorative gold band underneath the trophy; (above) two examples of how team winners are represented on the base of the award.

The Quebec senior league reached its apogee in the 1950s when
it provided a quality of hockey not far removed from the NHL or AHL.
Coach Punch Imlach got his start there, as did many future NHL
stars such as Jean Beliveau (with the Quebec Aces) and
Doug Harvey (with the Montreal Royals).

LADY BYNG TROPHY TO BOBBY BAUER

1940

THE NAME

Lady Byng was wife to Canada's Governor General who served Canada from 1921 to 1926. Lord Byng was commander of the Canadian Army Corps on the western front and played a key role in Canada's victory at Vimy Ridge in April 1917. Both Lord and Lady Byng attended Ottawa Senators games fervently, and to honour the league's most gentlemanly player Lady Byng gave a trophy to the NHL bearing her name.

THE TROPHY

Bauer's personal copy of the Lady Byng Trophy is an exact replica in miniature. The cup itself is only six inches high with small, simple side handles. The inscription identifies the trophy and his accomplishment: "Miniature of the Viscountess Byng of Vimy Challenge Cup/Presented by Viscountess Byng of Vimy to the National Hockey League 1935 to encourage clean sportsmanship/Won by Robert Bauer Boston Bruins 1939-40" The trophy sits on a small wood base.

WINNER

This mini version of the Byng Trophy was given to Bobby Bauer following the 1939-40 season. The tradition of giving a player a smaller version of the trophy is almost as old as the trophy itself, ensuring that the player possessed a keepsake for his accomplishments and to keep the original in circulation. A right winger, Bauer was the oldest member of the great Kraut Line that came out of Kitchener and led the Bruins to two Stanley Cups, in 1939 and 1941. Woody Dumart, the left winger, and Milt Schmidt, the centre, completed the line that remains the greatest in Boston history. It was Bauer's third full season in the NHL when he won his first Byng Trophy, and in a short period that threesome became the most potent line in the league until they all joined the Canadian war effort. Bauer also won the Lady Byng Trophy the next year, 1940-41, and again in '46-'47, his last full year in the NHL. He played one final NHL game five years later on the night the Bruins retired all three sweater numbers of the Kraut line, scoring a goal and an assist in a 4-0 win over Chicago on March 18, 1952. Bauer was successful at every level he played. He won a Memorial Cup with St. Mike's in 1934, and after two Stanley Cups in the NHL he returned to play amateur hockey during the war and won an Allan Cup in 1942 with the Ottawa Commandos, one of the greatest amateur teams of all time. After his playing career, he won two more Allan Cups as coach of the Kitchener-Waterloo Dutchmen (1953 and 1955), and then won a bronze medal at the 1956 Olympics in Cortina d'Ampezzo, Italy with Canada and a silver in 1960 in Squaw Valley. The Kraut Line was so famous that in 1959 the Bauer Krauts were formed, an Atom Triple A team playing in Kitchener that continues to represent that city as an all-star traveling team to this day.

The engraving on the trophy honours Bobby Bauer for his clean play in the 1939-40 NHL season with Boston.

The tradition of mini trophies being given to players is a long one and serves a dual purpose: On one hand, it ensures the original trophy is awarded in perpetuity; on the other, it allows the player a keepsake for his achievement.

SHIPSTADS & JOHNSON TROPHY

1944-1952

THE NAME

Eddie and Roy Shipstad and Oscar Johnson, founders of the famed Ice Follies, donated this trophy in 1944 to be given to the first place team in the Northern Division of the PCHL.

THE TROPHY

This huge and elaborate trophy seems excessive given its intentions and its brevity, but of course when a trophy is introduced the general feeling is that it will be around a while. The two-tiered base is made of wood, and on the four corners of both little bronze sculptures have been screwed into the wood. The lower four figures are hockey players while the upper four a more nebulous athlete with raised arms and garland in hand. The bottom section has nothing on its sides because there were so few winners that the plaques, which begin on the upper tier and consist of but a few names, have not all been used. The trophy in the middle is again large, though not particularly imaginative. It looks like a bigger and fatter version of the original Hart Trophy but on top is added a globe on top of which perches a spread-winged eagle.

GENESIS

The Pacific Coast Hockey Association was first started by members of the Patrick family in 1911. It was a seminal league in that it provided competition for the NHA and later NHL much as the WHA did in the 1970s, luring players from the east to the west and paying them as well as if not better than the NHL. The PCHA played on artificial ice and the players wore numbers on the back of their sweaters while playing with pioneering rules (such as the penalty shot). By 1924, however, it had disbanded as the NHL had established itself as the premier league in North America. In 1944, another professional west coast loop was established under the similar name of Pacific Coast Hockey League (PCHL), and to that end a series of new trophies was introduced. The Phil Henderson Memorial Trophy went to the league champion and the Southern California Trophy to the first place team in the Southern Division after regular season play.

FIRST WINNER

The Seattle Ironmen (sponsored by the Isaacson Iron Works, a local war production company) won the Northern Division in 1944-45 with a 20-6-1 record, their 41 points four ahead of second-place Portland. In the playoffs, they beat the Boston Olympics 4-2 in games to win the championship. The first four games were played in Vancouver. Boston won the first two, 5-4 (OT) and 8-5, but Seattle evened the series with wins of 11-4 and 10-4. The teams then returned to Seattle where the Ironmen completed the series victory with wins of 6-2 and 9-1. The high-scoring line of Frank Dotten-Johnny Ursaki-Shorty Coombs led the team all year, and young goalie Al Rollins was sensational from the first game of the season to the last for the Ironmen.

CHAMPIONS' HISTORY

Although the PCHL was primarily a two-division league, it struggled its final two years and consisted of just a few teams in one division from 1950 to '52, thus rendering the Shipstads and Johnson Trophy obsolete. The Ironmen and New Westminster Royals each won the trophy twice in its six years of existence, and three of the six winners went on to win the Henderson Trophy as well. The Royals also won during the final year of the trophy, 1949-50, defeating the Los Angeles Monarchs in a seven-game series, the last game going into overtime before the Royals won, 5-4. Their leading scorer was George Senick, who played a few games with the New York Rangers two years later, but his supporting cast was mostly non-NHLers who were at their peak playing in the PCHL.

TODAY

When the PCHL folded in 1952, all its trophies, of course, were retired. The Shipstads and Johnson Trophy made its way to the Hockey Hall of Fame where it has been part of the trophy collection for years.

(left) Details from the trophy's base reveal part of its charm as figures decorate the four corners of both the upper and lower tiers; (right) a detail of the top of the trophy.

Eddie and Roy Shipstad and Oscar Johnson were more famously known simply as Shipstads and Johnson, the creators of the Ice Follies. They started in 1934, producing a show for the Figure Skating Club of Minneapolis, and captivated the world over with their original and innovative ice dancing routines.

TURNER CUP

1945-2001

THE NAME

A native of Windsor, Ontario, Joe Turner was a goalie who rose to modest prominence during the war years, eventually playing his only NHL game for Detroit on February 5, 1942, in a 3-3 tie against Toronto to start for the injured Johnny Mowers. It was his only call-up from the minors that season. Soon after, Turner joined the U.S. Marine Corps, and nearly three years later he was killed in action while fighting in the Hentgen Forest in Germany on December 13, 1944. He was buried in a military cemetery in Belgium, and a decade later his remains were transferred home, to the Victoria Memorial Cemetery in Windsor.

THE TROPHY

The tallest and perhaps the simplest of the major trophies in the Hockey Hall of Fame's collection, the Turner Cup is made of wood and stands almost four feet high. A simple silver bowl rests on the top of an eight-tiered base, the tiers getting progressively bigger from the bowl to the ground. Like the Stanley Cup, each tier has a silver ring attached to it on which are engraved the teams and players names for each winning season.

GENESIS

Turner's finest moment came during that same 1941-42 season when he backstopped the Indianapolis Capitols to a Calder Cup victory. Shortly after his death, the Michigan-Ontario Hockey League evolved into the International Hockey League (IHL) and the governors, seeking to name their championship trophy, chose to honour Turner.

FIRST WINNER

The 1945-46 IHL featured just four teams—Detroit-Bright's Goodyears, Windsor Gotfredsons, Windsor Spitfires, and champion Detroit Auto Club. Coached by Jack Ward, the Auto Club featured players who never made it to the NHL and as such was an atypical champion team.

CHAMPIONS' HISTORY

For more than half a century, the IHL represented the third-best professional league in North America in a line that connected the NHL to AHL to IHL. In fact, by the 1990s, it might be said that the AHL and IHL were parallel in that a number of IHL teams had direct NHL affiliation in the chain of development that saw young players rise to the NHL. Turner-Cup winning coaches were also a who's who of both future NHL coaches and former NHL players, from Ebbie Goodfellow in '46-'47 to Fred Shero to Darryl Sutter, Butch Goring, and John Anderson. In the early years, the Cincinnati Mohawks were the dominant team, winning five championships in a row (1952-57) with players including Phil Goyette and Connie Broden. By the '90s, though, the league wasn't seen as a feeder league for the AHL; rather, it was an alternative for that league as a means of getting to the NHL on the way up, or as an alternative to Europe, on the way down. Theo Fleury was on the Turner Cup-winning Salt Lake Golden Eagles of '87-'88, Mark Recchi the next year with Muskegon, Sandis Ozolinsh with Kansas City in '91-'92, Tommy Salo a two-time winner (1994-96) with Denver and Utah, and Sergei Samsonov with the Detroit Vipers in '96-'97.

TODAY

As the 1990s advanced and the NHL expanded its reaches to every corner of North America, other minor leagues were affected. The AHL also expanded, searching for new, non-NHL cities to call home, and as a result the IHL had increasingly difficult a time to justify its existence. By 2001 it had closed its doors, a few teams joining with the AHL, the rest being disbanded. The Turner Cup, along with all of the IHL's archives, were sent to the Hockey Hall of Fame where these are preserved in perpetuity.

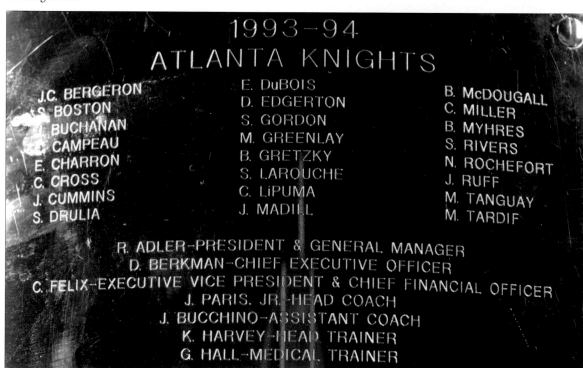

(left) A typical engraving of the winning team and its players and executive; (above) the name at the top of the trophy.

Now with eight bands of winning rosters, the Turner Cup has gotten bigger and bigger and is now the tallest trophy of its kind. The simple bowl at the top is augmented by tier after tier of wood with silver rings to accommodate the ever-expanding list of winners.

ART ROSS TROPHY

1948-PRESENT

THE NAME

A Hall of Famer and one of the longest-serving men the game has ever known, Art Ross followed a 14-year playing career that ended in 1918 with a life in hockey as coach and general manager, mostly with Boston, that lasted until 1955.

THE TROPHY

An ornate silver bowl with side handles sits atop a two-tiered wood base. The winners' names are engraved on round silver plaques that are attached to small pucks. The top base holds 24 pucks (six on each of the four sides), and the lower, bigger base holds 36 names (nine pucks per side).

GENESIS

Art Ross was an innovator as much as a great hockey player. He designed the goal net that was used by the NHL for more than half a century, and the Art Ross puck was the league's official puck for many years as well. He designed a helmet after Ace Bailey almost died from head injuries, and a protective piece for the Achilles tendon to prevent skate slashes to the back of the heel from becoming career-ending injuries. Ross believed that defencemen should be awarded points for saving goals, and he was instrumental in making several rule changes to improve the game. But perhaps his greatest idea was to give a trophy to the league's leading point getter each year. Ross and his two sons, Art Jr. and John, presented the trophy to the Board of Governors in 1948, the fifth individual trophy in the NHL's honour roll (along with the Hart, Lady Byng, Calder, and Vezina). The donation completed a program the NHL had started two years earlier when it gave the league's leading scorer a cheque for $1,000, the same amount as the other individual trophy winners. There are three ways to break a tie in the unlikely event two players have the same number of points: (1) the player who scores the most goals; (2) the player who has played in the fewest games; (3) the player who scores the first goal of the season. Only the first tie-break has ever been used (in 1979-80 when Marcel Dionne scored 53 goals to Wayne Gretzky's 51 after both finished the year with 137 points).

FIRST WINNER

In 1944-45, Elmer Lach finished first in points with 80 during the season that linemate Maurice Richard scored 50 goals in 50 games. The Rocket has just 23 assists and finished with 73 points in the pre-Art Ross Trophy days. In '47-'48, again playing on the great Punch Line with Richard on the right wing and Toe Blake on the left side, Lach again led the league in points with 30 goals and 61 points, just a single point better than Buddy O'Connor of the Rangers. This time, though, he received the first ever Art Ross Trophy for his fine season.

CHAMPIONS' HISTORY

There has always been tremendous cachet for the player who leads the NHL in points. Generally, such a player must combine excellent passing skills with pure, goal-scoring talent as well. The second-last player to win the Art Ross by scoring more goals than assists was Bobby Hull of Chicago in 1961-62 when he scored 50 times and had just 34 assists. In 2001-02, Jarome Iginla had 52 goals and just 44 assists in winning the scoring title. More incredible, when Peter Forsberg won in 2002-03 with 106 points, he scored just 29 goals, the fewest for an Art Ross winner since Ted Lindsay in 1949-50! Most incredible of all has to be Wayne Gretzky in the 1980s. In '82-'83, '85-'86, and '86-'87, he recorded more assists than the second-place point getter had total points, meaning he could have gone all season without scoring once and still would have won the scoring race! Needless to say, his ten career Art Ross Trophies is the most in league history.

TODAY

The Art Ross Trophy remains one of the pre-eminent awards of the NHL. The 2003-04 winner was Martin St. Louis of Tampa Bay, the third year in a row that a player had won the trophy for the first time (Forsberg won in '02-'03 and Iginla in '01-'02). What is even more incredible, however, is that the diminuitive St. Louis was never drafted! The 5'9" forward graduated from the University of Vermont in 1997 and played his way into the Calgary lineup after a year and a half in the minors.

(left) A detail of the bowl itself; (above) the puck and plaque for Bobby Orr, referred to as "Robert" at his mother's insistence!

The idea of incorporating pucks into a hockey trophy may be simplistic, but it is also surprisingly rare. No more effective use is there than the Art Ross, which has small silver plaques affixed to a puck for each year's winner. Take away the ornate handles and the bowl looks similar to the Stanley Cup bowl.

ST. MIKE'S MVP TROPHY TO TIM HORTON

| 1948 |

THE NAME

An award honouring Tim Horton after his first season of junior hockey at St. Mike's in 1947-48, this tiny, perfect trophy has no formal name.

THE TROPHY

Appropriately small for a high school award, this is the kind of award thousands of Canadian kids have stored in their basements or attics for some teenage accomplishment. It just so happens that the name on this trophy belongs to a future great defenceman. The half circle, wood base holds a simple, generic sculpture of a hockey player in action. The engraving is straightforward and has its place in history not because of what it represents but because of the name on it.

WINNER

Like so many players before and after him, Horton was recruited by the Leafs from the hinterlands. Cochrane, Ontario, was hundreds of miles from Maple Leaf Gardens, but owner Conn Smythe had scouts all across the land looking for talent, and in this small town they found Horton, a hulking defenceman with good skating ability and tremendous strength. Horton moved to Toronto to play junior hockey with the St. Michael's Majors, one of the two training grounds for future Leafs players (Toronto Marlboros was the other). Horton made a giant of an impression as a 17-year-old rookie with the Majors. He proved offensively capable and led the OHA in penalty minutes, and at season's end he was named the team's best player (thus this trophy). Horton joined St. Mike's during a time of transition, the Majors having just won the Memorial Cup for the second time in three years (1946-47). Amazingly, eight players were on both teams, notably Red Kelly (called Len at the time), Fleming Mackell, Ray Hannigan, Ed Sandford, Ed Harrison, Bob Paul, Howie Harvey, and Warren Winslow. In 1945, that Memorial Cup team had won 45 games and lost only four all regular season, and in the playoffs they had an unmatchable run, winning 14 consecutive games to clinch the national junior championship. The graduation of most of the team in 1947, however, left Horton playing with the more inexperienced likes of goalie Tommy Shea, defenders Bill McNamara and Bill Dunn, and forwards Peter Whelan, Joe Primeau Jr., and Jerry Fitzhenry. The result was a dismal placing of ninth in the ten-team league and missing the playoffs for the first time since 1940. In fact, the only players from this year's Majors team to go on to the NHL were Horton (1,446 games), Gord Hannigan (161 games) and Ray Barry (18 games). They were among the more than 150 Majors to play in the NHL, most of any institution anywhere in the world. Horton, who died in a single-car accident on the highway from Toronto to Buffalo on February 21, 1974, was one of a smaller number of St. Mike's alumni to be inducted into the Hockey Hall of Fame, yet his first signs of glory are represented by this small, high school MVP trophy.

Detail of the plaque honouring Tim Horton who came to Toronto to pursue a hockey career and get an education at the same time.

THE ONTARIO HOCKEY ASSOCIATION
MOST VALUABLE PLAYER AWARD
PRESENTED TO
TIM HORTON
ST. MICHAEL'S MAJORS
HOCKEY CLUB
SEASON 1947-1948

Tim Horton came out of Ontario's north to play for St. Michael's College in Toronto on his way to a pro career with the Maple Leafs. This was his first significant award and prefigured his remarkable, Hall of Fame career in the NHL.

DAVE PINKNEY TROPHY

1948-PRESENT

THE NAME

On February 11, 1948, Dave Pinkney was honoured at the Classic City Arena in Stratford for his contributions to the game in that town and in Ontario. By that time, he had been coaching at the Junior A level for nearly two decades, although he had started coaching as early as 1925 with a boys team in Stratford.

THE TROPHY

The Pinkney Trophy is wider than it is tall and made mostly of wood. It has three rectangular tiers of ever-smaller size from top to bottom, and on top of this third tier rests three columns of gold. The middle and widest column supports a goalie, and on the bottom tier, to the left and right sides, are similar goalies, representing the nature of the award for best goalie in OHA Junior A. Winners' names appear on individual plaques mounted along the sides of the bottom two wood tiers.

GENESIS

As part of its collection of individual trophies, the OHL awarded its best goalie every year with the Pinkney Trophy based on goals-against average.

FIRST WINNER

Gil Mayer of the Barrie Flyers was the first goalie to have his small plaque affixed to the Pinkney Trophy for his outstanding play during the 1948-49 season. Nicknamed "the Needle" because of his slight build, Mayer went on to play several games with the Maple Leafs between 1949 and 1956 during an otherwise excellent career in the minors. He played the first six seasons of pro mostly with the Leafs' affiliate, the Pittsburgh Hornets, and spent the next seven years guarding the goal of other AHL teams. Mayer won the Hap Holmes Award (the AHL's version of the Pinkney) an amazing five times in six years in the 1950s.

CHAMPIONS' HISTORY

Pinkney Trophy winners through the years include a who's who of greats and also-rans. Long John Henderson won with the Toronto Marlies in 1952-53, and two years later he was the starting goalie for the Bruins in Boston. Like Mayer, he went on to be a career minor leaguer, though not quite as accomplished. Dennis Riggin won in '53-'54 with the Hamilton Cubs, and Len Broderick won it in '57-'58, the same year he played his one and only NHL game as an injury replacement for Jacques Plante in the Montreal goal. He allowed just two goals in a 6-2 win over Toronto on October 30, 1957. Gerry Cheevers won with St. Mike's in 1959-60 just before embarking on what would be a Hall of Fame career as did Bernie Parent with the Niagara Falls Flyers five years later. Jim Ralph, a goalie who went on to become much more famous as a broadcaster, won with Ottawa in 1980-81. More recent NHLers who won the Pinkney include Kevin Hodson, who had a 28-12-4 record with the Soo Greyhounds in '91-'92 before joining the Red Wings and winning a Stanley Cup in '97-'98. Dan Cloutier won in '95-'96 with Guelph Storm teammate Brett Thompson in '95-'96, and in 2003-04 Gerald Coleman and Ryan MacDonald of the London Knights shared Pinkney honours. Their NHL careers have yet to be determined, but if history has proved anything, they'll at least get a chance to prove themselves at the highest level.

TODAY

The Pinkney continues to be handed out every year by the OHL along with a raft of other individual awards including the Eddie Powers Memorial Trophy (top scorer), Max

Kaminsky Trophy (best defenceman), and Red Tilson Trophy (most valuable player). In 2004-05, Adam Dennis and Gerald Coleman won the Pinkney Trophy as they back-stopped the London Knights to a remarkable year, allowing a mere 125 goals in 68 games to set an OHL and CHL record. The team lost just seven times all year and captured the Memorial Cup.

(left) A golden goalie is part of the design of the Pinkney; (above) the name engraved on the body of the award; (below) a sampling of winners' plaques that appear on the side of the wood base.

The Pinkney Trophy has remained in use for more than half a century, honouring the best goalie in the league. The 2004-05 winners, not surprisingly, came from the dominating London Knights, Memorial Cup champions.

TUROFSKY TROPHY

1949-1972

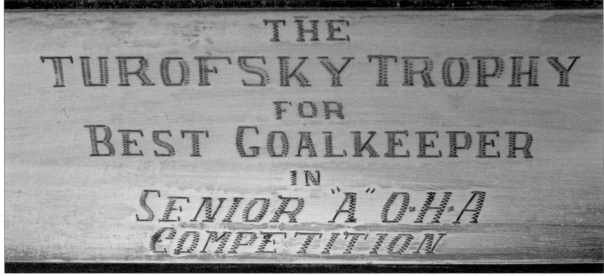

THE NAME

Brothers Lou and Nat Turofsky were the most important hockey photographers for nearly 40 years. They were stationed every game night at Maple Leaf Gardens, and their images were reproduced in every newspaper across the country. Their large-format, black-and-white images, made with flashes and strobes, represent the greatest documentary achievement of Original Six hockey.

THE TROPHY

The four corner pillars that form the core of this trophy quickly recall the Vezina Trophy, and the fact that both are awarded for goalies lends further credence to the comparison. But the pillars are crowned by a simple, silver helmet on top of which stands, oddly, a skater, not a goalie. Too, within the pillars stands another skater, not a net as with the Vezina, or a goalie to symbolize the nature of the award. The one-piece wood base holds the winners' names on small silver plaques. The trophy wasn't in circulation long enough to fill this single wood base.

GENESIS

Such was the popularity of the Turofskys, and their importance to the game, that the OHA named their best goalie trophy after the brothers. Initiated in 1949, it remained in circulation in Senior hockey until 1972.

FIRST WINNER

Marcel Pelletier of the Kitchener-Waterloo Dutchmen won the first Turofsky Trophy for a season that included a league-best GAA of 2.65. It turned out to be fitting tribute to a

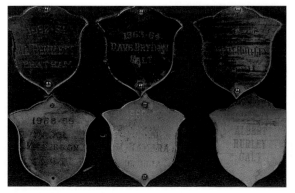

career minor leaguer, for Pelletier was just starting a life on goal that lasted nearly 20 years and almost as many teams. His NHL totals amount to just eight games, six with Chicago in 1950-51 and two more a dozen years later with the Rangers. He had a 1-6-0 record and allowed nearly five goals a game, far higher than his career numbers in the minors. Beyond that, Pelletier played mostly in the WHL, notably with the Victoria Cougars.

CHAMPIONS' HISTORY

In February 1973, the Turofsky Trophy found its rightful home when it was given over to Harold "Boat" Hurley at a special ceremony in Galt. During a 20-year career, Hurley won the award an unprecedented eight times, starting in 1951-52 with the Kitchener-Waterloo Dutchmen. He won it again the next year with the Dutchmen and a third time in '57-'58. Hurley won it consecutively in '60-'61 and '61-'62 with the Galt Terriers and again with the Guelph Regals (1964-66). He won it for the last time in his second-to-last season of active play, 1970-71, with the Galt Hornets. Many consider Hurley to be the greatest goalie never to play in the NHL.

TODAY

Like so many other important trophies, the Turofsky Trophy made its way to the Hockey Hall of Fame after it was removed from active circulation by the OHA. Hurley was its last recipient.

(left) Plaques from the side of the base acknowledge winners; (above) detail of the identifying plate; (right) close-up of a skater—not goalie—that stands at the top of the best goalie award.

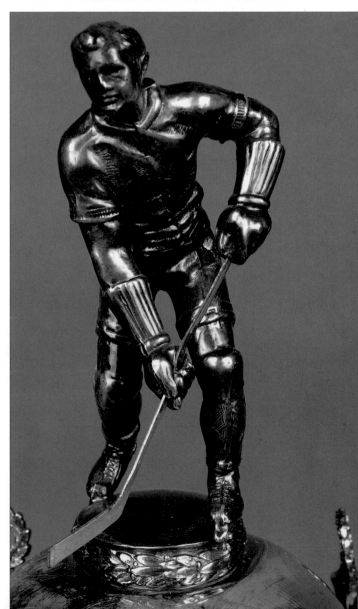

The Turofsky Trophy
for
Best Goalkeeper
in
Senior A OHA

Over the years, a few non-playing men have been honoured with
trophies in their name, but Lou and Nat Turofsky are surely the
only photographers so honoured. Their remarkable careers at
Maple Leaf Gardens paved the way for the trophy designation.

1953 WORLD CHAMPIONSHIP TROPHY

1953

THE NAME

Unlike many of hockey's great trophies, the World Championship cup is not named after a man whose contributions to the game are memorialized on the trophy itself. Simply, it is the honour bestowed by the IIHF upon the winning nation of the most important international tournament.

THE TROPHY

One of many trophies the IIHF has presented over the years to the winner of the annual World Championship, this is among the smallest and lightest. The wood base has one plaque on it, bearing the names of winners from 1953-59. The silver cup is long and thin, with Art Deco-like handles and inscribed only with the IIHF logo of the day.

FIRST WINNER

The year 1953 marked the first time ever that Tre Kronor, the name ascribed solely to Sweden's national hockey team, won gold at the World Championship. Held in Zurich and Basel, Switzerland, the 20th edition of the tournament featured but four teams—Sweden, West Germany, Switzerland, and Czechoslovakia. Furthermore, the Czechs pulled out of the competition midway through to mourn the passing of their president Klement Gottwald. As a result, the three surviving teams all made it to the medal podium, the first and only time this has happened in the history of the championship. Nevertheless, Sweden finished with a perfect 4-0-0 record. The team was led by superstar forwards Sven "Tumba" Johansson and Hans Oberg.

CHAMPIONS' HISTORY

Tre Kronor won the gold again four years later, in 1957 when the tournament was held in Moscow. That was a more formidable victory, for it was clinched on the last day because of a 4-4 tie with the host nation Soviets. The Soviets had joined the IIHF only in 1954 and shocked the hockey world by defeating Canada 7-2 to win gold on the final day in their first appearance. It was only the third time in 34 years that Canada failed to win gold in an international event it had participated in. Nonetheless, the Canadians rallied in 1955 as the Penticton V's, the country's representatives that year, finished the tournament with a perfect 8-0-0 record, including a 5-0 whitewash of CCCP on the last day. The Vees outscored the opposition 66-6 in that 1955 world championship and were backstopped by Don Moog in goal (his son, the more famous Andy, played many years in the NHL). Up front, the team featured the great Warwick brothers—Bill, Dick, and Grant. The Soviets again upset Canada in 1956 to win Olympic gold in Cortina d'Ampezzo, but after Sweden's win in 1957 (to protest the Hungarian Invasion by the Soviets in 1956, Canada did not compete), the Canadians won the next two tournaments. In 1958, in Oslo, Norway, the Whitby Dunlops claimed gold by compiling a perfect 7-0-0 record and outscoring their opponents 82-6 with a team led by captain Harry Sinden. Roy Edwards and Long John Henderson were the goalies and other stars on the team included Connie Broden, John MacKenzie, and J-P Lamirande. The next year, the team successfully defended its title in Czechoslovakia losing only once in eight games, to the Czechs on the final day when they were already assured of gold. J-P Lamirande was on that team as well, a rarity of the day because different club teams from across Canada represented the nation each year, so the likelihood that one player would be on consecutive teams was virtually nil. Other notable players on the '59 team included Red Berenson, Moe Beaoit, and Pete Conacher.

TODAY

After winning the World Championship in 1959 for the third time since the inception of this version of the trophy, Canada was given it for good and the IIHF introduced a new one for the 1961 World Championship. It was not until 2001 that the IIHF introduced one trophy to be presented annually to the winning nation.

(left) From the side of the trophy, the stylized "IIHF" is engraved to give it official status; (below) detail of the only plaque indicating winners up to the time the trophy was given to Canada.

WINNERS
1953 - SWEDEN
1954 - CCCP
1955 - CANADA   PENTICTON V'S
1956 - CCCP
1957 - SWEDEN
1958 - CANADA - WHITBY DUNLOPS
1959 - CANADA - BELLEVILLE McFARLANDS

It was not until 2001 that the IIHF crafted a World Championship trophy that would be presented annually to the winning nation. Previously, different trophies were made each year or, in earlier days, the same trophy was in use until one nation won it three times.

EDINBURGH TROPHY

1954-1957

THE NAME

His Royal Highness, the Duke of Edinburgh, donated this trophy to the Canadian Professional Hockey Champions in March 1954. He and Princess Elizabeth (soon to be Queen Elizabeth) had visited Canada in 1951 and had been so impressed by Canada's winter game that he donated a trophy bearing his name.

THE TROPHY

The Edinburgh Trophy was minted by Henry Birks and Sons from a design by a group of artists, a design approved by the Duke himself. It features a hockey player made of silver mounted on a silver globe with a map of North America (like most sculpted skaters with sticks, this player shoots right!). The wide, ebony base bears the Dominion coat of arms, and small plaques for the names of winning teams are added to the side of the base all around. On top of the base the words "THE EDINBURGH TROPHY" appear. This is one of the most imaginative and enjoyable trophies in the collection.

GENESIS

The Edinburgh Trophy was awarded to the winner of the national playoffs between the winners of the Quebec Hockey League versus the Western Hockey League, two professional leagues below the NHL and AHL. It was the pro equivalent of the Allan Cup, emblematic of amateur champions of

Canada. The QHL had changed from an amateur to professional outfit only a year before and was without a championship trophy. Previously, the QHL champions competed with the Maritime Hockey League to play for the Alexander Trophy, donated by Lord Alexander, another former Governor General, but when the QHL became pro, the Alexander Trophy slipped into retirement.

FIRST WINNER

The Calgary Stampeders beat the Quebec Aces 5-1 in a best-of-nine series to win the first Edinburgh Trophy. All games were played in Alberta (five at the Corral in Calgary, one in Edmonton). Game One was close for a period, the teams being tied 1-1 after 20 minutes, but the Stamps ran away with the game by scoring seven unanswered goals and winning 8-1. Two days later, the Aces tied the series with a 2-1 victory, but then it was all Calgary the rest of the way. Game Three was the turning point. The Stamps won a thriller 6-5 in a game in which no team led by more than a goal at any time. The Aces twice pulled their goalie late and almost tied the score, but this Calgary win took the steam out of the QHL champions' sails. The Stamps won the next game, 7-4, and the game after, 2-1, and in Game Six they overcame an early 2-0 deficit to win 4-2.

CHAMPIONS' HISTORY

The Shawinigan Cataracts beat Edmonton 5-2 in 1955 and the year after the Winnipeg Warriors were the victors. In 1957, it was the Aces that won, but this was the last time the

trophy was up for competition. The year after, when it was the West's turn to host the championship series, the WHL declined the honour because of late playoffs in the WHL and PCHL intended to avoid conflicting with the Stanley Cup playoffs. In succeeding years, many suggestions were presented to revive the Edinburgh Trophy playoffs, but none resulted in its re-introduction.

TODAY

There is no formal professional championship within Canada any more. The Allan Cup remains the most important and longest surviving trophy after the Stanley Cup, and teams competing for the Allan have paid players on their rosters. Pro leagues across North America have sprung up in every city imaginable, but the relevance of the Edinburgh Trophy has long passed and it now is on display at the Hockey Hall of Fame, testament to an era long passed.

(left) Detail of the coat of arms of the Duke of Edinburgh; (above) the name as it appears on the top of the base; (right) a winning team's name as it appears on the trophy.

Although at first glance the trophy appears to be part of something larger, the Edinburgh Trophy is very much its own entity, the silver globe and player very much an impressive design element on top of a footstool base.

JAMES NORRIS MEMORIAL TROPHY

1953-PRESENT

THE NAME

A native of St. Catharines, Ontario, James Norris was the longtime owner and president of the Detroit Red Wings. He bought the franchise in 1932 after having made his millions in the grain and shipping industries. It was he who changed the nickname of the team from Falcons to Red Wings.

THE TROPHY

The Norris Trophy consists of a silver bowl with lid, unadorned, sitting atop two octagonal-shaped tiers. The lower tier is wider than the upper, but both contain the same number of long, narrow, silver plaques onto which are engraved winners' names. Each of the eight sides holds five names, so the trophy in total will have 80 winners when it is full in its present form.

GENESIS

Shortly after the death of Norris in 1952, his four children presented a trophy in their father's name to the NHL, to be given annually to the best defenceman in the league.

FIRST WINNER

If ever there were such a thing as an under-rated hall of famer, Red Kelly fits the bill. He won four Stanley Cups with Detroit as a defenceman in the 1950s, and four more with Toronto as a centre in the 1960s. He won the first Norris Trophy for his play in 1953-54, a year in which the Wings won their third of four Cups in a five-year span.

CHAMPIONS' HISTORY

As puck is to hockey, so Orr is to Norris. But before the legendary Bruins defenceman there was Montreal's Doug Harvey, who won the trophy seven times in the first nine years of its existence. However, when Harry Howell of the Rangers won in '66-'67, he said this: "I'm glad I won it this year. For the next few years they'll have to rename it the Bobby Orr award because that young man in Boston will own it." Indeed, Orr won it for the next eight successive years, the only man to win as many individual trophies in a row, in any sport. As much as any trophy, the Norris is an award for eras and moves in cycles. After Orr, it was handed down to Denis Potvin and Larry Robinson, and then Orr's proteges, Paul Coffey and Ray Bourque, won it several times. Nicklas Lidstrom in Detroit was runner-up three years in a row (1997-2000) before winning it three consecutive years. For virtually its entire history, it has been considered an award to honour offensive ability by a defenceman. Perhaps only Rod Langway, who won in 1982-83 and again the next year in Washington, was a true stay-at-home blueliner to win Norris recognition. This is not to demean the defensive abilities of any of the winners, only to say that the first words that those names evoke from a fan have to do with scoring, skating, and generating offense, rather than play inside their own blueline. Brad Park holds the unenviable record of having been runner-up six times, four when Orr won and twice more when Potvin took the honours.

TODAY

The 2003-04 winner was Scott Niedermayer of New Jersey. Much like Al MacInnis in '98-'99, this seemed to be a career trophy rather than recognition for an outstanding year in '03-'04. Niedermayer has been in the NHL since 1991 but had never won an individual award despite winning three Stanley Cup championships, an Olympic gold in 2002 with Team Canada, and a World Cup in 2004. If anyone deserved an honour for a great career, it had been first MacInnis and then Niedermayer.

(left) The engraving as it appears on the bowl of the trophy; (above) a sampling of the Norris domination by Bobby Orr, who won the trophy for eight successive years. Harry Howell of the Rangers won it in 1966-67 and Denis Potvin in '75-'76. In between, it was all Orr.

Like teams and eras, the Norris Trophy has been subject to dynasties during its history. Doug Harvey won it seven times in eight years, Pierre Pilote three in a row, Bobby Orr eight straight, and Ray Bourque four times in five years.

MINI STANLEY CUP TO CONN SMYTHE

1955

THE NAME

The Stanley Cup has been in existence since 1893, awarded annually to the champions of the NHL playoffs since 1927.

THE TROPHY

There is nothing fancy about this trophy except that it is a miniature version of the greatest trophy of them all, the Stanley Cup. Gold, it has smaller ribbons of barrels and an engraved dedication to him for his achievements during a 30-year career in Toronto. The Cup also features each team—players and all—who won a Cup under Smythe's guidance, seven in all.

WINNER

This personalized trophy was given to Conn Smythe by Happy Day, his longtime colleague and friend at Maple Leaf Gardens, to recognize the unparalleled contribution made by Smythe to the NHL and hockey in Toronto. Dated February 18, 1955, it represented the official retirement of Smythe as team general manager and the introduction of Day as his replacement. Smythe bought the Toronto St. Pats in 1927 and immediately changed the team's nickname to Maple Leafs. He organized the building of Maple Leaf Gardens in just six months in 1931, the

height of the Great Depression, and during his career he turned the Gardens into the hockey capital of the world. Smythe hired Foster Hewitt as broadcaster, so that fans from "coast to coast" could follow the Leafs, and gave Lou and Nat Turofsky run of the place to take photographs and spread the gospel of the team through images. He began feuds with other GMs to stir controversy and thereby generate fan interest in the four American NHL cities. He hired bird dogs (scouts) to ensure that his team signed the best players in the country. Smythe also turned the Gardens itself into a place of constant development and progress. He filmed games and practices as early as the 1940s, installed Plexiglas and a modern clock above centre ice. He set up a Press Room second to none and made sure fans in the high-priced seats (reds and blues) dressed in suits and gowns appropriate for the opera or concert hall. His mini-Stanley Cup is testament to all these, but, most important, honours the seven Cups he won with the team as its owner, president, GM, and leader.

CHAMPIONS' HISTORY

Two other mini Stanley Cups were soon after given to great men of the game. In 1961, Tommy Ivan received one in Chicago, in part to honour his three Cups with Detroit (1949-50, 1951-52, 1953-54), but mostly to thank him for delivering the Hawks their first championship since 1938 (which he had just done in the spring of '61). A year later, Jack Adams received a mini-Cup for his lifelong contribution to the Detroit Red Wings, one that included seven league titles in a row (first place) to go with seven Stanley Cups during an affiliation that lasted some 35 years.

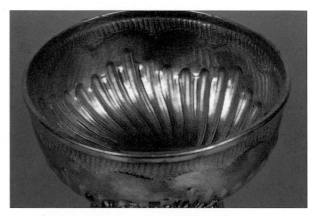

(left) The dedication to Conn Smythe as it appears near the base of the mini Cup; (top) the inside of the bowl is pristine, unlike the real Cup which is full of scratches from years of celebrations; (above) the list of Cup teams that Smythe created, complete with roster names and members of the executive.

A little more than a foot high, this truly is a mini version of the Stanley Cup. The gold trophy, made in the image of the great gift of Lord Stanley, has been conferred to few men whose lifetime contributions merit such gratitude.

TROPHY TO GEORGE HAYES

1959

THE NAME

George Hayes was the first man to officiate 1,000 NHL games, a feat he accomplished on March 21, 1959.

THE TROPHY

An award made for a specific person and a specific achievement, this accommodates all the necessary information to convey the purpose of the honour. The base holds a dedication on a gold plaque, and the tall body holds the game puck from Hayes's historic game and his whistle. At top, a more generic element, a hockey player, refers to Hayes's sport, though he was not known as a player or skater.

CLARENCE CAMPBELL
CARL VOSS
"KING" CLANCY
BILL CHADWICK
"BUTCH" KEELING
RED ARNOTT
RED STOREY
FRANK UDVARI
EDDIE POWERS
SAM BABCOCK
LOU FARRELLI
GAYE STEWART
BILL MORRISON
ART SKOV
MATT PAVELICH
ROGER STRONG
NEIL ARMSTRONG
JACK MEHLANBACHER
BILL ROBERTS
MILT SCHMIDT
HECTOR DUBOIS
HAMMY MOORE
MAX SILK
FRANK UPTON
CLAUDE ROSE
BILL McLAUGHLIN

GENESIS

This award was given to Hayes on behalf of his colleagues, the other referees and linesmen of the NHL to commemorate one of their own.

FIRST WINNER

Hayes led a rebellious life outside the arena, so it goes without saying his was a colourful career in the NHL. He began to officiate in 1936 as a youngster, working his way up to the OHA five years later and the AHL in 1943, a career climb made faster by the war. In 1945, with the best officials back in game action, Hayes was back in the OHA where he finished the season as a referee in the Memorial Cup. Soon after, he signed with the NHL and began as a referee, but he argued frequently with league president Clarence Campbell and happily took a demotion that made him a linesman. At 6'3" and 220 lbs., Hayes was, literally, head and shoulders above most of the players with whom he skated alongside and as such was effective during rough moments of games. He worked long after receiving this plaque, leaving the game in February 1965 after he refused to take an eye exam. "I told him [NHL President Clarence Campbell] there was nothing wrong with my eyesight. I told him I kept testing them by reading the labels on liquor bottles in Dinty Moore's bar in Montreal." Unimpressed, Campbell fired him. Hayes had worked 1,544 regular-season games, 149 more in the playoffs, and eleven All-Star Games. It was thought that because the NHL president considered him a "rebel" that Hayes would forever be refused entry into the Hockey Hall of Fame, but in 1988 he became the eleventh inductee into the Officials' category in recognition of his contributions to the game.

TODAY

The Hayes family donated the trophy along with numerous of his scrapbooks to the Hockey Hall of Fame. The trophy, adorned with the game puck and whistle used during that historic 1,000th game, is unique and fitting tribute for a man who survived the officiating wars in the NHL for some 19 seasons.

(left) The back side of the trophy lists the donours; (top right) detail of Hayes's whistle; (middle right) the puck from game number 1,000; (bottom right) the inscription from the trophy's base.

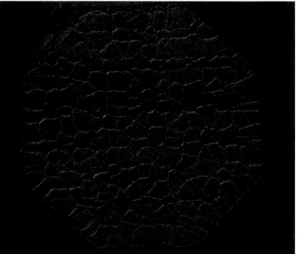

A trophy created especially for George Hayes, this lifetime achievement honours his 1,000 games as an NHL official and as such includes the whistle and a puck from that historic game. These are mounted on a unique trophy topped by a small gold bowl and a hockey player.

SPENGLER CUP

1950-1961

THE NAME

Dr. Carl Spengler (1860-1937) of Davos, Switzerland donated a trophy in his name in 1923 for competition between German and Austrian national teams and the best club teams in Europe. He achieved his doctorate in 1886 and began the study of tuberculosis in Strassburg. He returned home to Davos in 1889 to study with his father and later succeeded his father as director of a prominent sanatorium in Davos.

THE TROPHY

A decorative, small, gold goblet, this version of the Spengler Cup was handed over to the first team that won the tournament three times in a row. This happened in 1961 after Paris ACBB won for the third time. Each year's winner from 1950 to '61 is engraved on a gold plaque that is nailed to the square, wood base. The goblet itself has the name of the tournament engraved on it, and the top is a decorative, moveable lid.

GENESIS

As a result of World War I, the International Ice Hockey Federation (IIHF) banned Germany and Austria from sanctioned, international competition. To fill the void, Dr. Spengler created a trophy for a tournament that would allow those nations to compete at a high level. Thus was born the Spengler Cup, which is still contested every year from Christmas Day to New Year's Eve in Davos, featuring five teams (four top clubs in Europe and a makeshift national team from Canada).

FIRST WINNER

This trophy, the third version of the Spengler Cup, was first minted for the 1950 tournament, won by HC Diavoli Rosso Neri from Italy.

CHAMPIONS' HISTORY

The home team had an excellent run in the 1950s with this trophy, winning three times (1951, 1957, 1958) under the leadership of Pic Cattini, first as a player and then as coach. Fussen (1952), Milano (1953, 1954), and Ruda Hvezda Brno (1955) also won before the end of the decade, but it was Paris ACBB (Athletic Club de Boulogne Billancourt) that had the greatest glory, winning three times consecutively (1959-61), a feat accomplished only twice previously. As a result of this Spengler dynasty, the team was given this trophy after the third victory, in 1961, and the tournament crafted a new one for the 1962 winners (Spartak Praha).

TODAY

When the Hockey Hall of Fame opened its international zone in 1998, thanks to its strengthened affiliation with the IIHF in Switzerland, this Spengler Cup, along with hundreds of other artifacts and historical pieces, became an important part of the new exhibition space.

(left) Detail of three winners of the trophy from 1953, '54, and '55; (above) detail of the body of the trophy.

The Spengler Cup is presented to the winner of a Christmas week tournament that has a life all its own. Teams from various countries compete in a round robin series of games to qualify for a one-game finals, the winner having its name on the Cup. Three wins by any team means that team gets to keep the trophy and a new one is crafted.

ADAMS CUP

1963-1984

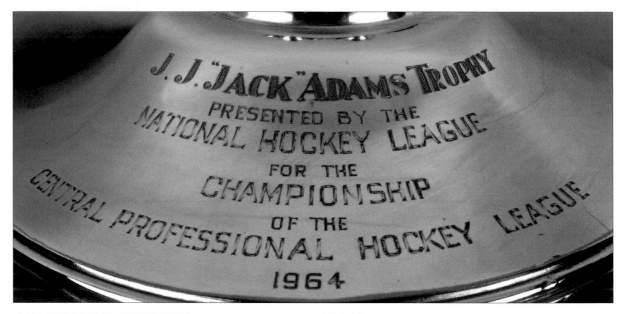

THE NAME

Over a 35-year career, Jack Adams was the greatest success in the history of the Detroit Red Wings, first as a coach and then general manager, having a hand in the team's first seven Stanley Cup victories (1936, 1937, 1943, 1950, 1952, 1954, 1955).

THE TROPHY

This round trophy has two tiers of wood painted black supporting a gold-coloured trophy in the shape of a sort of flame. The two parts of the base have small plaques with winners' names on them, and the trophy is without inscription except for the top of the flat cover which indicates its importance.

GENESIS

Jack Adams was named the first president of the Central Professional Hockey League (CPHL) in 1963, a rubric used until 1969 when it became simply the Central Hockey League (CHL). Adams helped found the league and wanted it to become the prime professional developmental league for the NHL. To that end, he mandated that each team could have only one player over 25 years of age and three over 23; the rest of the roster had to be younger than 23, to give young players a professional league in which to develop their skills. It was a league that ranked above the junior level but below the top-flight of NHL. Each of the four teams in the league had direct affiliation with an American-based NHL team of the Original Six: Omaha (Detroit), Minneapolis (Boston), St. Louis (Chicago), and St. Paul (New York). Because of Adams's importance to the NHL and the fledgling league, the Adams Cup was named to honour the league's playoff champions. Even though the trophy is engraved "Adams Trophy" it has long been known as the Adams Cup.

FIRST WINNER

The Omaha Knights beat St. Paul in five games of their best-of-seven at the end of the 1963-64 season. The Knights had Ernie Wakely in goal, and six of the top dozen point-getters in the league were from that team: Bob Courcy, Garry Peters, Len Ronson, Barclay Plager, Bill McCreary (playing coach), and Doug Senior.

CHAMPIONS' HISTORY

During its 21 seasons of existence, the CHL developed dozens of future NHL stars and gave hundreds of lesser players a league to play in. In 1971, goaltender Michel Plasse helped make the league famous when he fired the puck into the empty net at the other end, becoming the first goalie in pro hockey to score a goal. In the 1982 playoffs, another future NHL star, Kelly Hrudey, was named MVP of the post season, and in earlier years the stats charts were full of names that became NHL recognizable. Glen Sather and Terry Crisp played for the champion Oklahoma City Blazers in '66-'67; Pat Quinn helped Tulsa win the next year. Other alumni of the CHL include Phil Esposito, Mike Vernon, Rogie Vachon, Gerry Cheevers, and Serge Savard. The Omaha Knights are the only franchise to win the Adams Cup four times. Tulsa, Dallas, and Salt Lake have all won three times.

TODAY

The original Adams Cup found its way to the Hockey Hall of Fame more than a decade after the original CHL ceased operations. When a new CHL emerged in 1992, that league introduced a redesigned Adams Cup to be awarded to the league champions of the regular season while starting a new trophy (William Levins Trophy) for the playoff champions. A short time later, however, the league abandoned the Adams name altogether and gave the top team after the regular season the Governors' Cup while the playoff champions received the Ray Miron President's Cup.

(above) Detail of the trophy's dedication from the lid of the bowl; (below) winning teams have their names engraved on small silver plaques nailed to the side of the base.

The importance of Jack Adams to the success and development of the NHL and minor hockey in the U.S. cannot be over-stated, so the naming of the CPHL championship trophy came as no surprise to anyone in the game when the Adams Cup was created in 1963.

CONN SMYTHE TROPHY

1965-PRESENT

THE NAME

Conn Smythe was the longtime owner and president of the Toronto Maple Leafs. After buying the Toronto St. Pats in 1927, he changed the team's nickname to "Maple Leafs" and made it the most popular team in the country. In 1931, he financed the building of Maple Leaf Gardens, and within six months a new arena stood on the northwest corner of Church and Carlton Streets in downtown Toronto. For more than 30 years Smythe oversaw every aspect of the building's and team's operation.

THE TROPHY

A gorgeous and delicate trophy among the NHL's awards, the Conn Smythe features a silver replica of Maple Leaf Gardens presented on a backdrop of a huge silver maple leaf. Three wood tiers sit underneath this silver temple of hockey, all containing winners' names which are engraved on stylized silver maple leaves. As of 2005, it has five blank leaves for future winners after which the Hockey Hall of Fame will have to decide whether to add a new base or how else to create more room for winners' names. Perhaps more than any other, this trophy conveys its inspiration and provenance.

GENESIS

By the early 1960s, Conn Smythe had more or less sold the Leafs and had nothing to do with the day-to-day operations of the club. To honour his life in hockey and, more specifically, his contributions to the game in Toronto and Canada,

the Board of Directors of Maple Leaf Gardens donated a trophy to the NHL to be given to the best playoff performer every year. The trophy is designed in the shape of the Gardens with a giant maple leaf acting as a dramatic curtain behind the building. Today, Maple Leaf Gardens is the only Original Six building still standing.

FIRST WINNER

Jean Beliveau, captain of the Montreal Canadiens, won the first Conn Smythe Trophy in May 1965 after leading his team to a seven-game victory over Chicago in the Stanley Cup finals. He recorded 16 points in 13 playoff games that spring en route to his sixth of a remarkable ten career Stanley Cup wins.

CHAMPIONS' HISTORY

More than any other trophy, there is enormous sentimentality attached to the Conn Smythe. It's about honouring the best player over a short but utterly grueling stretch of games. As is fitting, goalies have won 12 of the 40 editions of this award. Patrick Roy is the only three-time winner (1986, '93, and 2001), and Bernie Parent (1974 and '75) and Mario Lemieux (1991 and '92) are the only players to win it consecutively. The list of players to win the trophy while playing for the losing side in the finals is just five

names long: Roger Crozier (Detroit, 1966), Glenn Hall (St. Louis, 1968), Reg Leach (Philadelphia, 1976), Ron Hextall (Philadelphia, 1987), and J-S Giguere (Anaheim, 2003). Montreal goalie Ken Dryden made history when he won in 1971 with just six career regular-season games under his belt, the only player to win playoff honours before winning the Calder Trophy. Because it is a modern-era trophy, expansion teams are well represented among the winners. Montreal players have won the Conn Smythe Trophy nine times, but Detroit, Edmonton, the Islanders, and Philadelphia have all had four winners.

TODAY

The Conn Smythe Trophy is voted on by members of the Professional Hockey Writers' Association and is not without its controversial moments. When J-S Giguere won in 2003, for instance, no one could have disputed his remarkable playoffs, but many did consider Martin Brodeur's performance to be as good—and he played for the winning team! Few could argue with Brad Richards's nomination in 2004 after he scored a record seven game-winning goals of his team's 16 victories en route to Tampa Bay's first Stanley Cup. Richards, in just his fourth NHL season (all with Tampa Bay), also led the playoffs with 26 points.

(left) The dedication to Smythe on the side of the trophy; (above) the elaborate and beautifully detailed silver replication of Maple Leaf Gardens, the house that Smythe built.

As the NHL has expanded and the playoffs have grown into a four-round marathon, the Conn Smythe Trophy has become evermore important in honouring the best playoff performer. In Smythe's day a player might play 14 playoff games at the most; today, he can play as many as 28.

ATHOL MURRAY MEMORIAL TROPHY

1966-1990

THE NAME

Monsignor Athol Murray, known to one and all simply as "Pere" has perhaps had a direct hand in developing more pro hockey players—and more tremendous men—than anyone involved in the sport from the day the puck was invented. Born in Toronto, he was ordained there in 1918 and nine years later wound up in Wilcox, Saskatchewan as parish priest. Six years later, he established Notre Dame of Canada, a liberal arts college affiliated with the University of Ottawa. During the Depression years, Pere Murray often accepted

flour, meat, or coal as tuition payment for the children attending. He established not only an educational institution of the highest calibre but he extended the college's offerings to include sports, principally hockey. Over the years, he developed dozens of young boys into NHL-playing men, and those who played hockey but didn't succeed at the NHL level most often went on to enjoy commensurate success in the working world. In 1981, the Legislative Assembly of Canada formally accepted the college's name change to read Athol Murray College of Notre Dame, such was the admiration everyone who attended felt for him and his singular contributions to its success.

THE TROPHY

An admirer of this trophy wouldn't have a clue what it represented without the plaques on it, for the simple silver trophy in the middle of a two-tiered base is without engraving or inscription. The pot-bellied trophy features an ornate symbol of victory on top, and the small square base that supports this has a plaque bearing Monsignor Murray's name and the trophy's intent. Below is a very wide wood base that carries the winning teams' names on its four sides. Two hockey players stand on guard to the side of the trophy, resting on the wide, main base.

GENESIS

In 1966, the Western Canadian Junior Hockey League (later, the WHL) started its own premier junior league and named its championship trophy in the memory of Pere Murray.

FIRST WINNER

The Moose Jaw Canucks were by no means the best team in the league during the 1965-66 regular season. They finished fourth in the seven-team WCHL with a 25-19-12 record, 16 points behind the front running Edmonton Oil Kings. But although the Oil Kings averaged a goal and a half more per game, they were virtually identical in goals against. In the

playoffs, the teams met in the now-unusual best-of-nine semi-finals series, and Moose Jaw won three games and lost two; the teams tied four times. Amazingly, the favoured Oil Kings were out and the Canucks were on their way to the finals. Once there, they beat the Estevan Bruins 4-1 in a more traditional best-of-seven series to win the first Athol Murray Trophy. Players from that team included Jim Booth, Gary Bredin, Bill Comrie (father of Mike and Paul), Ken Hodge (not the NHL Hodge—this Hodge suffered an eye injury that ended his career), and Barry Long.

CHAMPIONS' HISTORY

The New Westminster Bruins won four successive championships (1974-78), the last two leading to Memorial Cup wins as well. The first WHL team to win the Memorial Cup was the Regina Pats in 1973-74, and in the mid- to late-1980s the WHL ruled the junior ice lanes in Canada, winning four national championships in five years. Prince Albert won in '84-'85, and then Medicine Hat won back-to-back titles in 1987 and '88. The next year, Swift Current kept the western dynasty going, winning the Athol Murray Trophy and Memorial Cup one after the other.

TODAY

In 1990, a new trophy named Presidents' Cup was minted and replaced the Athol Murray Trophy, which was sent to the Hockey Hall of Fame to help celebrate Pere's contribution to the game in perpetuity.

(left) Detail of one of the silver hockey player miniatures that bookend the wood base of the trophy; (above) names of winning teams as they appear on the trophy.

It is perhaps the strangest piece of trophy trivia in the collection that the plaque bearing the trophy's name is spelled incorrectly! Pere Murray's first name has but one "l" in Athol, but the inscription gives it two—Atholl!

LESTER PATRICK TROPHY

1966-PRESENT

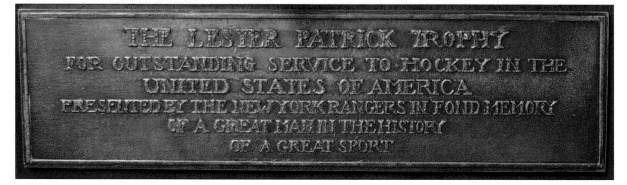

THE NAME

A native of Drummondville, Quebec, Lester Patrick played the game for many years before becoming coach of the Rangers in 1926, a position he held for 14 years during which time the club won two Stanley Cups. In all, he spent more than half a century in the game and was the patriarch of one of hockey's greatest families. Two of his sons, Muzz and Lynn, played in the NHL, and two of Lynn's sons, Craig and Glenn, also made the pros in the NHL.

THE TROPHY

From the bottom of the wood base to the top of the Patrick's head that is the statue, this 7' "trophy" is by far the largest in the Hall of Fame's collection. The sculpture features Patrick wearing practice attire and guiding players on ice as a coach. The large wood base has plenty of room to accommodate honourees, each of whom has a narrow strip of bronze nailed to the base for dedication.

GENESIS

In 1966, six years after Patrick's death, the New York Rangers donated a trophy to honour their great coach and GM. It was to be given "for outstanding service to hockey in the United States," and was open to players, coaches, executives, officials, and referees, and journalists.

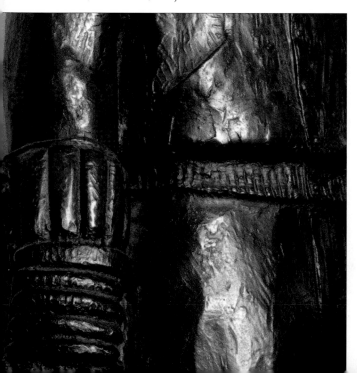

FIRST WINNER

Of course, any trophy that begins in 1966 has plenty of catching up to do, so Jack Adams, retired coach and GM of the Detroit Red Wings was the first recipient, an award he could have won two decades earlier had it been around then. Adams built the Detroit franchise from nothing to Cup winners seven times, and under his stewardship it became the soundest franchise in the United States. No more deserving recipient could have been chosen to start the Patrick Trophy history.

CHAMPIONS' HISTORY

More than any trophy, the list of Patrick winners is a mixed bag of players and non-players, well-known and little known. Yes, the names of Orr, Gretzky, and Howe grace the Patrick, but so too do Jim Hendy, Bob Fleming, and Larry Pleau, to name a few. The selection committee for the Patrick Trophy consists of Gary Bettman (as NHL commissioner), a representative of the Rangers, an NHL governor, a member of the selection committee from the Hockey Hall of Fame in both the Player and Builder categories, a member of the U.S. Hockey Hall of Fame, a member of the NHL Broadcasters' Association, and a member of the Professional Hockey Writers' Association. Each year all positions are rotated, except Bettman's. As a result, Charles Schulz, the creator of Peanuts and a huge hockey fan, was recipient in 1981. Men such as Frank Mathers and Murray Armstrong, who had pedestrian NHL careers as players but went on to coach successfully for many years in the U.S., are also recipients. Unlike the Hockey Hall of Fame induction honours, the Patrick Trophy can also be awarded to teams, something that has happened three times. In 1980, that year's gold medal men's team—the Miracle on Ice team—was so honoured; in 1999 the U.S. women's Olympic team of the previous year was honoured for winning gold for the first time at a major tournament; and in 2002, the 1960 the U.S. men's Olympic team, the only other American gold medalists, were given their due.

TODAY

Winners in 2004 reflect the breadth and range of contribution to the game in the U.S. Ray Miron, active in hockey for half a century, was one winner; John Davidson, a broadcaster notably with Madison Square Garden Network was the second honouree; and, Mike Emrick, longtime play-by-play voice for fans in the U.S. completed the list Patrick Trophy winners.

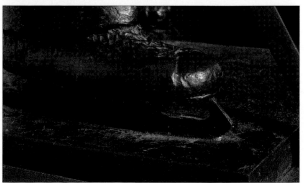

(left) Detail from the trophy; (top) the dedication plaque; (above) a partial list of winners as they appear on the large base beneath the sculpture, and a detail of the skate from the trophy.

The original trophy is larger than life, standing more than 6' high, but the replica given to each winner is less than a foot high. Nonetheless, the Lester Patrick Trophy honours a man whose career in New York was extraordinary and as such is fitting title for people who have made outstanding contributions to hockey in the United States.

CLARENCE S. CAMPBELL BOWL

1967-PRESENT

THE NAME

Clarence Sutherland Campbell was the NHL's president from 1946 to 1977 during which time he revised the game in every conceivable way, from the number of teams in the league to the rules to the very design of the Stanley Cup itself.

THE TROPHY

One of the biggest and most ornate of the NHL's trophies, the Clarence Campbell Bowl is a large, sterling silver tankard mounted on a hexagonal base. The jug features ornate embellishments on all elements of it except for a flat band around the midriff of the bowl wherein the name of the trophy in inscribed. It is only on the base that winning team's names are engraved in equally ornate silver plaques.

GENESIS

In the ever-expanding era of the NHL following 1967, the Campbell Bowl was introduced in that year in which the league doubled in size from six teams to 12. The top team in the East Division at the end of the regular season was awarded the Prince of Wales Trophy while the West Division champs won the Campbell Bowl. Previously, the Prince of Wales had been awarded to the league champs when it was a one-division, six-team league, but with expansion it became a divisional award and the introduction of a similar trophy for the West Division became necessary.

FIRST WINNER

During the last three days of the 1967-68 regular season, the Clarence Campbell Bowl was very much up for grabs. Philadelphia and Los Angeles both had 71 points, but the Flyers had three games remaining and the Kings just one. The Flyers beat St. Louis 2-0 on March 28, and the next night the Kings managed only a 2-2 tie with lowly Oakland. Philadelphia lost both its remaining games, but that single point was the margin of victory for the Flyers. The team also received a cash sum of $47,250, based on 21 equal shares of $2,250 each.

CHAMPIONS' HISTORY

As the East and West Divisions expanded again in 1970, 1972, and 1974, it became clear a two-division league was quickly becoming outdated. To begin the '74-'75 season, president Campbell realigned the teams into four divisions under two larger umbrella conferences, the Prince of Wales and Campbell, in honour of the trophies. As such, the winner of the Campbell Conference at the end of each regular season won the Campbell Bowl, and this format continued until 1981 when it was awarded to the winning playoff team from that conference. In 1993, when NHL Commissioner Gary Bettman stripped the divisions and conferences of their names and renamed them for geographic regions in the hopes of making the game more appealing to American fans, the Campbell Conference became the Western Conference, consisting of the Central Division and Pacific Division. The winner of that still received the Clarence Campbell Bowl. In 1998-99, the league continuing to expand, each conference now had three divisions (as it does today), but still the top team in the Western Conference playoffs (i.e., the Western representative in the Stanley Cup finals) received the Campbell Bowl. In the first decade of use, the Flyers won the Bowl six times, and in the 1980s, of course, it was Edmonton and Calgary that dominated. In the 1990s, Detroit became the most powerful team in the West.

TODAY

The 2003-04 Calgary Flames became perhaps the unlikeliest winner of the Campbell Bowl as they marched to the Cup finals with three impressive series victories. They beat Vancouver in overtime of game seven in the opening round of the playoffs, stunned Detroit in six games in the conference semi-finals, and finished their work by beating San Jose in six games to get to their first Cup finals since winning it all in 1989.

(left) Ornate medallions grace the side of the base of the bowl for each year's winner; (below) the inscription on the bowl indicating the trophy's purpose.

CLARENCE S. CAMPBELL BOWL
Presented by the Member Clubs
for Perpetual Competition
by the
National Hockey League
1968

The base of this trophy holds 55 names, so the Hockey Hall of Fame still has plenty of time to decide what to do when all medallions have been filled with winning teams' names.

BILL MASTERTON TROPHY

1968-PRESENT

THE NAME

Bill Masterton was an NHLer whose life ended as a result of a check during a game on January 13, 1968. He struck his helmetless head on the ice after colliding with an opponent and died in hospital two days later.

THE TROPHY

Because this is a modern trophy, introduced long after most of the league's significant individual honours, the Masterton Trophy deviates from the common perception of what a hockey trophy should look like. In this case, it has the standard wood base with names engraved on small, silver plaques, but above the trophy itself consists of three silver torches of varying heights in which are held gold flames (to signify that although Masterton may have died, the flame— his memory— carries on). The square wood base has its corners cut off to create smaller flat sides upon which some of the winners' names can be affixed.

GENESIS

Just days after Masterton's death, the annual All-Star Game took place in Toronto, but there was little talk of superstar moves and fancy passes or great glove grabs. All the buzz was about helmets and whether they should they be made mandatory. In light of Masterton's death, who would voluntarily wear a helmet? To recognize the tragedy of a life lost, and to fill a void in player honours, the Professional Hockey Writers' Association created the Masterton Trophy to be awarded annually to the player "who best exemplifies the qualities of perseverance, sportsmanship, and dedication to hockey."

FIRST WINNER

Hard working. A checker. Unsung. Solid at both ends of the ice. Those are some epithets given Claude Provost of the Montreal Canadiens upon the announcement he had won the first Masterton Trophy at the end of the '67-'68 season, a vote which included the nomination of some 21 players.

CHAMPIONS' HISTORY

In retrospect, we see that this was, more than any other, a nascent set of criteria for the Provost honours. Quickly the

Masterton Trophy became known more for what we say today is a worthy Masterton candidate—someone who has overcome a serious physical illness or injury to play the game at the highest level. In 1972, Bobby Clarke was given the Masterton in recognition of his success at the NHL level while dealing with diabetes on a daily basis. The next year, Lowell MacDonald won in recognition of his return to the game despite several serious knee injuries. Oddly enough, Bobby Orr never won the Masterton, though Brad Park, with equally wobbly knees, did win in 1984 at the end of his great career. Tim Kerr and Gord Kluzak won for their fights with shoulder injuries, and Mario Lemieux was given the Masterton in 1993 when he battled Hodgkin's disease to return to the NHL at the height of his powers. Gary Roberts won for his amazing comeback from a serious neck injury, and in 2000, New Jersey's Ken Daneyko won not for a fight with an injury but rather a sickness. He battled the bottle, and with the help of the league's substance abuse program returned to the game as a Cup-winning defenceman again. In 2003, Steve Yzerman won the Masterton for his extraordinary ability to play through excruciating pain in his knee, undergo a rebuilding of that knee, and return to the game as good as ever.

TODAY

The 2003-04 Masterton winner was Bryan Berard of Chicago, and for anyone who saw the horrific eye injury he suffered as a Maple Leafs defenceman playing in Ottawa midway through the 1999-2000 season, it is an honour much deserved. Berard's career seemed over—even his

insurance company agreed—but he refused to retire, refused to accept a $6 million cheque from that insurance company. He underwent numerous surgeries, and although he remains virtually blind in one eye, he came back to be an effective defenceman again, much to the amazement and admiration of all.

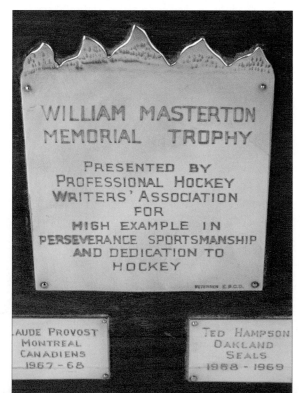

Details from the base of the trophy indicating its purpose and honouring the winners. Claude Provost of Montreal was the inaugural winner, receiving the honour just months after Masterton's death.

The flames in this trophy, gold and brilliant, never go out. Neither does the spirit Masterton brought to the game or by which he is remembered, the only player to have died as a result of injuries sustained during an NHL game. Each winner of this award has provided as much inspiration to fans as any goal or victory.

CENTENNIAL CUP

THE NAME

The Centennial Cup was given to Canadian Junior A hockey by the city of Winnipeg in honour of its 100th birthday.

THE TROPHY

A smaller and simpler version of the Stanley Cup, the Centennial Cup has four tiers of silver rings which support an unadorned bowl on top. Each tier has the names of winning teams with rosters, like the Stanley Cup, but each winner appears on a small plaque that is attached to the ring rather than engraved directly on it. The bowl has two ribbon-like handles and only the trophy's name engraved on it.

FIRST WINNER

The Red Deer Rustlers beat the Charlottetown Islanders in P.E.I. to win the first ever Centennial Cup. In those days, until 1978, the top two teams from regional playoffs faced each other in a seven-game series. Red Deer won in six games, and one of the stars on the team was Perry Pearn who has since gone on to have a fine coaching record in junior hockey. One of the top players on the local Islanders was future NHLer Al MacAdam.

CHAMPIONS' HISTORY

The provincial Junior A leagues have two main functions: (1) to provide top-level hockey for junior-aged players who can't make the CHL or who choose not to play there; (2) to provide a level of purely amateur play for players who wish to go on to play NCAA hockey in the United States. The Centennial Cup has seen many great NHLers, notably Paul Kariya, James Patrick, Rod Brind'Amour and three of

TODAY

There were three versions of the Centennial Cup. This silver edition was introduced in 1994 and lasted just two years. In 1996, the name changed to the Royal Bank Cup, and with it came a new trophy. All three Centennial Cups eventually were donated to the Hockey Hall of Fame.

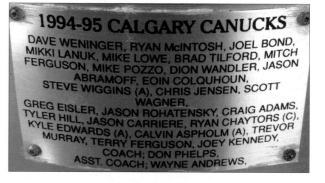

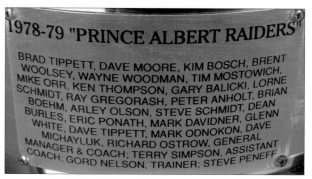

(left) Detail of the name engraved on the bowl; (above) three examples of how teams and names are honoured on this third version of the Centennial Cup.

GENESIS

By 1971, the Memorial Cup was still the only trophy competed for nationally by junior-aged players. The introduction of the Centennial Cup was a long overdue way to bring together regional winners to play in one tournament to determine a Canadian champion. The regional winners played for various trophies to qualify for the Centennial play-downs. In Alberta and B.C., the Doyle Cup winners advanced. In Manitoba and Saskatchewan, it was the Anavet Cup winners, and in Quebec, central Ontario, and the Maritimes, teams played for the Fred Page Cup. Northern and Southern Ontario had the Dudley Hewitt Cup.

the Sutter brothers (Brent, Rich, Ron) who led Red Deer to victory in 1980. Brind'Amour and goalie Curtis Joseph led the Notre Dame Hounds to victory in 1988. Coach Terry Simpson led the Prince Albert Raiders to three Centennial Cups (1977, 1979, 1981). Including both the Centennial and Royal Bank Cups, Vernon, British Columbia is the only team to win four times (twice while called the Lakers, in 1990 and '91) and twice as the Vipers ('96 and '99). Besides Simpson's teams, only Guelph, Thunder Bay, and Red Deer have won even twice. Given the number of provincial junior teams in Canada, the Centennial Cup is, in some ways, the hardest hockey trophy to win.

Crafted in the spirit of the Stanley Cup, this is one of three versions of the Centennial Cup, and it in turn was replaced by the Royal Bank Cup in 1995. Regardless what it's called or what it looks like, its place in provincial Junior A hockey remains important and secure.

LESTER B. PEARSON AWARD

1971-PRESENT

THE NAME

Canada's 14th prime minister, Lester B. Pearson is the only Canadian to win the Nobel Peace Prize, in 1957, after he created the United Nations peacekeeping force a year earlier during the Suez Crisis.

THE TROPHY

The two parts of this trophy are oddly dissimilar. The bottom is a triangular base, hollow and light, weighing no more than a couple of pounds. The top is a bronze of a hockey player weighing more than 20 lbs. The lower part consists of the trophy name on one panel and winners' names on the other two. Underneath the player on the top is an angled platform representing ice and speed as he comes to a stop, turning sideways and using both skates.

GENESIS

The NHL Players' Association introduced the Pearson at a press conference on March 10, 1971. "The winner will be decided by a secret ballot among all of the association

1995-96	MARIO LEMIEUX	PITTSBURGH PENGUINS
1996-97	DOMINIK HASEK	BUFFALO SABRES
1997-98	DOMINIK HASEK	BUFFALO SABRES
1998-99	JAROMIR JAGR	PITTSBURGH PENGUINS
1999-00	JAROMIR JAGR	PITTSBURGH PENGUINS
2000-01	JOE SAKIC	COLORADO AVALANCHE
2001-02	JAROME IGINLA	CALGARY FLAMES
2002-03	MARKUS NASLUND	VANCOUVER CANUCKS
2003-04	MARTIN ST. LOUIS	TAMPA BAY LIGHTNING

members (i.e., all NHL players)," NHLPA executive director Alan Eagleson said in making the announcement. "The plaque will go to the player who has contributed the most to hockey." It is the only trophy the players have a hand in determining a winner and as such has enormous prestige. The Hart Trophy, its MVP companion piece, as it were, is voted on by members of the Professional Hockey Writers' Association, and frequently over the years a player who wins one also wins the other in any given year. This is the second version of the trophy, introduced in the early 1990s.

FIRST WINNER

While defenceman Bobby Orr won the Hart Trophy in 1970-71, it was teammate Phil Esposito who won the first Pearson Award. Either trophy could have gone either way, but there was no player close to these two, this year. Esposito set individual league records by scoring 76 goals and 152 points, and Orr became the first player ever to have 100 assists in a season (102) to go with a record 37 goals by a blueliner. The pair had led the Bruins to the Cup in 1970 but this year they were stymied by Montreal in the quarter-finals, losing in seven games.

CHAMPIONS' HISTORY

Only 12 times in the history of the Pearson Award has the winner been different than the Hart Trophy recipient. Interestingly, seven of those anomalies came in the first eleven years of the award's inception, suggesting that over time the two opinions started becoming one. Throughout the 1990s, each year saw the same player win both the Hart and Pearson, although the 21st century has seen a shift back to the early days when voices differed. In 1999-2000, Jaromir Jagr (Pittsburgh) won the Pearson although Chris Pronger (St. Louis) won the Hart (in one of the closest races ever); in 2001-02, Jarome Iginla (Calgary) was honoured by his colleagues while the sportswriters chose Montreal goalie Jose Theodore; and, the next year Markus Naslund (Vancouver) was the best according to the players while the writers opted for Swedish compatriot Peter Forsberg (Colorado). Only two goalies have ever won the Pearson, Mike Liut (St. Louis) in 1980-81, and double winner Dominik Hasek (Buffalo) in 1996-97 and again the next year. The Hart has a similar penchant for avoiding the crease, having given itself over to only six goalies since its inception in 1923-24. Wayne Gretzky is the only five-time winner of the Pearson (in a six-year period, 1981-87), four of those coming consecutively. Guy Lafleur (1975-78) is the only other player to

win it three successive seasons. Mario Lemieux won it four times, but perhaps more amazingly is that those wins took place over a span of eleven years, winning first in 1985-86 and last in '95-'96, and never twice in succession. Mark Messier is the only player to win it with different teams, in 1989-90 when he led the Gretzky-less Edmonton Oilers to the Stanley Cup and two years later with the New York Rangers. Toronto and Chicago are the only two Original Six teams not to have a Pearson winner on their roster.

TODAY

The Pearson is now more than thirty years old and is an established part of the annual silverware handoff. That the players still vote on it remains its greatest charm and importance, and it remains an integral part of the Hockey Hall of Fame's Great Hall displaying the greatest hockey trophies of the NHL.

(far left) The most recent winners as they appear on one of the triangular sides of the trophy; (near left) detail of the top of the award.

It is the Hart Trophy as voted on by the players themselves, and many consider being named the league's best player by those they play with and against the greatest honour in the game. For that reason, the Lester B. Pearson Award holds a special place in the NHL's annual trophy celebration.

AVCO WORLD TROPHY

THE NAME

Named after a financial services company, the trophy was ridiculed at the time for its affiliation with a sponsor, but in today's NHL of arena sponsorships, the AVCO trophy now merely seems way ahead of its time. AVCO stands for Aviation Corporation of America.

THE TROPHY

The AVCO Cup, as it is more commonly called, was designed by Don Murphy of Toronto and features a silver cup on a black, ironwood base. Only the team names and years of victory are engraved on small silver squares nailed to the base. The centerpiece of the trophy is a silver globe which floats in a crystal casement between the cup above and the base below, symbolic of the international character of the WHA. The cup itself is plain silver without much adornment.

GENESIS

The WHA was all about money and about luring dissatisfied, underpaid NHLers to a league of commensurate quality with modern salaries. When the league started in 1972, it needed a championship trophy to compete with the Stanley Cup, and AVCO stepped up as a sponsor and a cash donation of $500,000 for naming rights.

FIRST WINNER

On May 6, 1973, the New England Whalers defeated the Winnipeg Jets 9-6 in game five of their best-of-seven finals to win the first AVCO World Trophy. The team included many fringe NHLers from years gone by, notably former Calder Trophy winner Brit Selby of the Leafs, another former Leafs forward, Brad Selwood, and WHA rookie of the year Terry Caffery who had played 14 games with Chicago and Minnesota in the NHL (1969-71). Other players from that team included Tommy Williams, Tom Webster, Rick Ley, Al Smith, and Jim Dorey. The night of the victory, the trophy had not yet been crafted, so it wasn't until the summer that the Whalers received the cup.

CHAMPIONS' HISTORY

The AVCO World Trophy was won seven times. After New England in 1973, the Houston Aeros won it for the next two years. This was a team featuring the father-sons trio of Gordie Howe and children Marty and Mark and another handful of lesser-rans from the NHL. The Winnipeg Jets won in 1975-76, its first of three wins featuring the first great international line of Bobby Hull playing with Swedish stars Ulf Nilsson and Anders Hedberg. In '76-'77, the Quebec Nordiques won. Jim Dorey was on that team, and its biggest stars were captain Marc Tardif, J.C. Tremblay, and Real Cloutier.

TODAY

The trophy in the Hockey Hall of Fame is one of three AVCO Cups. A second is in Winnipeg, the last team to win it, and a third is at the Nova Scotia Hall of Fame having come from AVCO's head offices (its president was a Nova Scotian). Of course, when four WHA teams merged with the NHL in 1979 (Edmonton, Calgary, Hartford, Quebec), thus disbanding the WHA, the trophy ceased active importance.

(left) A detail from the side of the cup; (below) this surreal globe floats in the middle of the trophy.

THE
AVCO
WORLD
TROPHY

The first hockey trophy sponsored by a business, the AVCO Cup, as it was known, presaged many trophies, honours, and arena names which also receive sponsorship from corporations to promote the game and its licensees.

LOU KAPLAN TROPHY

1972-1979

THE NAME

Lou Kaplan was a trustee and chairman for the Minnesota Fighting Saints during the inaugural season of WHA play (1972-73) and an important supporter for bringing a franchise to the city.

THE TROPHY

One of the more enigmatic trophies, this rookie of the year award consists of two simple elements: a perfectly square, black wood base and a slightly larger than life gold hockey glove. The base has only one gold panel on its side with the names of the only winners (the WHA existed only from 1972-79), and the glove is hollow with the fingers pointing down into it.

GENESIS

With the introduction of the WHA in 1972, the league had to create a series of trophies to honour the best players and teams annually. While the AVCO Cup was given to the champions of the playoffs, the Lou Kaplan Trophy was awarded to the rookie of the year. However, because the league was created as alternative to the NHL and in most cases teams stocked their rosters with disgruntled NHL players, "rookie" is a misnomer and perhaps "first year player" is a more apt description of the award's merit and relevance.

FIRST WINNER

Terry Caffery was the trophy's first recipient, although he was anything but a rookie. By the start of the '72-'73 season, he had played three years of professional hockey. In 1969-70, the Chicago draft choice from 1966 played six games with the Hawks in a year he spent mostly with the farm team in Dallas in the CHL. The next year, Caffery was traded to the Minnesota North Stars, and again played just a few games with the NHL team in an otherwise minors season. The next year, he played solely in the AHL, and with little prospect of making an NHL team full-time he signed with the New England Whalers, where he played for three seasons.

CHAMPIONS' HISTORY

During the seven seasons the WHA existed it produced an impressive list of first-year players to win the Kaplan Trophy. In '73-'74, the honour went to Mark Howe, the 18-year-old who defied the NHL's draft rules (which prevented players under 20 from being drafted) and signed with the Houston Aeros so that he could play with his brother, Marty, and father, Gordie. The next year, Kaplan Trophy winner Anders Hedberg made history by leaving his Swedish team with another Swede, Ulf Nilsson, to join Bobby Hull in Winnipeg as the first, truly international line, a high-scoring threesome that gave the WHA exposure and life as an entertaining, skilled league. In '75-'76, it was Mark Napier who joined the Toronto Toros and promptly scored 43 goals with his great speed and hard shot to win the rookie of the year. It was his only major individual award in his career, but he also won the Stanley Cup with Montreal (1978-79, his first NHL year) and Edmonton (1984-85). Lesser-known George Lyle won

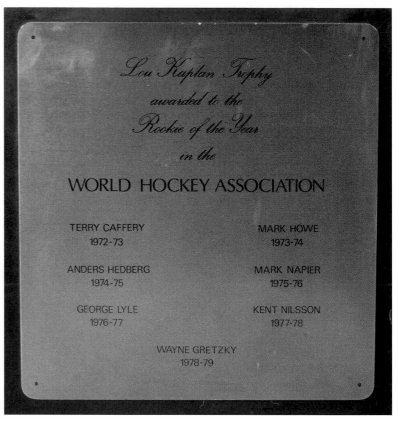

Lou Kaplan Trophy
awarded to the
Rookie of the Year
in the
WORLD HOCKEY ASSOCIATION

TERRY CAFFERY	MARK HOWE
1972-73	1973-74
ANDERS HEDBERG	MARK NAPIER
1974-75	1975-76
GEORGE LYLE	KENT NILSSON
1976-77	1977-78
WAYNE GRETZKY	
1978-79	

the next year, and then Kent Nilsson, whom Wayne Gretzky later called the most skilled player he had ever seen, recorded 107 points in his first WHA season to win the award. The last year of the WHA's existence, 1978-79, it was Gretzky himself who won, having been wooed to Edmonton by Nelson Skalbania. The 17-year-old #99 had 46 goals and 110 points in his tuneup season for the NHL. Once in the NHL, Gretzky failed to win a major individual award only five of his 20 years in the league.

TODAY

Of course, when the WHA merged with the NHL in the summer of 1979, the WHA's trophies became purposeless and were all retired to the Hockey Hall of Fame.

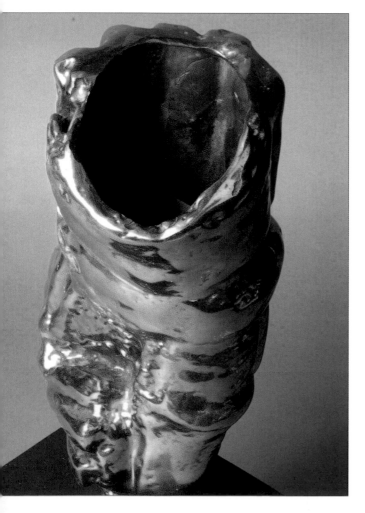

(left) The trophy is faithful to its design as a glove insofar as one can put a hand in it all the way to the fingers; (top) all winners' names fit onto one sheet of gold which takes up one side of the wood base.

*Not many hockey awards are designed from equipment, but the
Lou Kaplan is one such example. The gold glove of hockey lasted
only as long as the WHA before being retired and finding its
way to the Hockey Hall of Fame.*

JACK ADAMS AWARD

1973-PRESENT

THE NAME

Jack Adams began as a player with the Toronto Arenas in the first year of the NHL in 1917, but he became the stuff of legend through some 35 years' association with Detroit as coach and general manager.

THE TROPHY

Another multi-tiered trophy, the Jack Adams Award is the simplest of the NHL's major individual honours. The two lowest wood tiers hold plaques bearing the names of the honoured coaches, the top consisting of 18 names, the larger, lower tier holding 22 plaques. Between these and the silver bowl rest an almost square base that is as high as the two lower tiers combined. It holds a larger plaque bearing the trophy's dedication. The bowl above has ornate handles and relief at the bottom but is otherwise without inscription. The lid handle at the top also serves to hold a portrait of Adams resembling a hockey card made of silver.

GENESIS

From 1927 to 1947 Jack Adams coached the Red Wings and made every player move associated with the team. He led the team to three Stanley Cups, and in the '50s, as Detroit general manager, won four more. If ever a coach of the year award was to enter the NHL in honour of one man, no one was more deserving than Adams. The Jack Adams Award came to the league in 1974 as a gift from the NHL Broadcasters' Association.

FIRST WINNER

As its first recipient, Philadelphia's Fred Shero was as controversial a choice as any in the history of this honour. Sure enough, he led the Flyers to a Stanley Cup in 1973-74,

THE JACK ADAMS AWARD
COACH OF THE YEAR

PRESENTED ANNUALLY TO THE NHL COACH ADJUDGED TO HAVE CONTRIBUTED THE MOST TO HIS TEAM'S SUCCESS BY THE NHL BROADCASTERS ASSOCIATION IN MEMORY OF THE LATE J.J. (JACK) ADAMS WHOSE LIFETIME DEDICATION TO HOCKEY SERVES AS AN INSPIRATION TO ALL WHO WOULD ASPIRE TO FURTHER THE GAME.

J.J. (JACK) ADAMS
1895 – 1962

1976 - 77
SCOTT BOWMAN
MONTREAL CANADIENS

but he did so with a team that fought and intimidated its way to victory, means virtually everyone in the hockey world condemned.

CHAMPIONS' HISTORY

No trophy elicits jibes and jokes as much as the Adams, for although its prestige cannot be questioned, brethren realize that coaches are, as the saying goes, meant to be fired. As such, there is a superstitious feeling that whoever wins the award will soon be fired. Pat Burns is the only three-time winner of the Adams, and he did so with three Original Six teams— Montreal in 1988-89, Toronto in '92-'93, and Boston in '97-'98. Jacques Demers is the only man to win consecutive honours, and he did so both times with Detroit (1986-88). Pat Quinn and Scotty Bowman are the only other two-time winners. Because of the nature of the award, the Adams often does not go to a coach who goes to the finals or wins the Cup. Instead, those men who are seen as doing a great job with a minimum of talent, or taking the club up several notches in the standings, are frequently winners. In fact, only three

times has the Cup-winning coach won the Adams: Shero, in the inaugural year, Scotty Bowman in '76-'77, and John Tortorella, in 2003-04 with his incredible Tampa Bay Lightning. One team achievement does seem mandatory, though, and that is making the playoffs. No coach has won the Adams without reaching the 'second season.'

TODAY

No Adams Award winner is still coaching the team for which he won that honour, with the exception of Tortorella (last year's winner), and Jacques Lemaire (winner the previous season). The rule of 'what have you done for me, lately?' is more applicable to coaches than any other person in the game, and although a coach may have a good season with a team, the trophy carries no weight or influence when his team starts to lose.

(far left) The plaque honouring Scotty Bowman; (above) silver plate dedicating the trophy to Adams; (near left) the top of the trophy with a playing card-style photo of Adams.

By definition, the Jack Adams Award is both a blessing and a curse, blessing because it is a coach's finest honour, curse because every man to have been so honoured has, at some point, been fired by his team! That's what coaching is all about.

BILL HANLEY TROPHY

1975-PRESENT

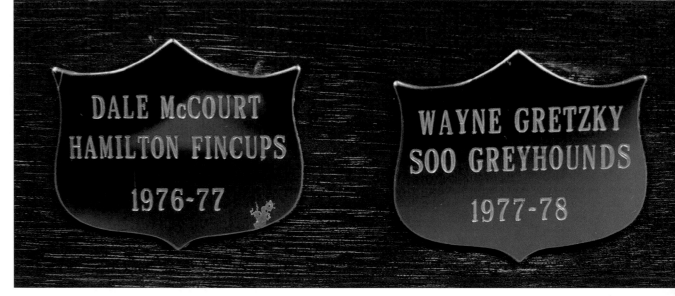

THE NAME

Bill Hanley worked as secretary-manager of the OHA for some 27 years. He succeeded W.A. Hewitt, Foster's father, in 1947 and oversaw much of the post-war era of junior hockey. Hanley had started his career in the family's butcher business after being discharged from the Royal Canadian Navy after the war. When he was asked by Spiff Evans, an employee of Conn Smythe, to become penalty timekeeper at Maple Leaf Gardens, he accepted without regrets. Hanley moved into the OHA as its assistant business manager, preparing statistics and performing other league duties, and worked his way up as the league expanded and required more of his tremendous organization skills.

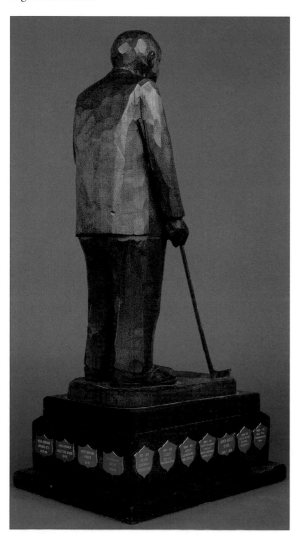

THE TROPHY

This is a rare example of a trophy in the Hockey Hall of Fame's collection that is made entirely of wood. The three thin parts of the base are all pieced together, but the sculpted portrait of Hanley that sits above these parts is made of one piece of wood, with the exception of the hockey stick which was glued to his hand after the body was finished. Since Hanley was an executive rather than a player, he is depicted not in the traditional hockey equipment but rather a jacket and tie.

GENESIS

When Hanley retired in January 1975, the OHA held a special dinner in his honour at the Westbury Hotel in Toronto. Among the gifts and special surprises for "Mr. OHA," as they called him, came the announcement that starting immediately the Max Kaminsky Trophy for the league's most gentlemanly player would be renamed the Bill Hanley Trophy, and it has stayed that way ever since.

FIRST WINNER

Doug Jarvis capped a superb junior career with Peterborough by recording 138 points in '74-'75 and winning the first Hanley Trophy as well. He was drafted by Toronto that summer of 1975, but the Leafs traded him to Montreal before he ever played a game in the blue and white. Jarvis then went on to become the NHL's all-time Iron Man, playing in 964 consecutive games. As important, Jarvis continued his sportsmanlike play at the highest level, recording only 263 career penalty minutes in those 964 regular season games.

CHAMPIONS' HISTORY

Considering this is a lesser trophy at the junior level, it is impressive how many names on the Hanley Trophy have gone on to make a significant impact on the game at a higher level. Dale McCourt won the award twice in the mid-1970s, and Wayne Gretzky won in '77-'78, his only year of junior hockey. Kirk Muller won while playing for Guelph in '82-'83 and, of greater surprise, the feisty Mike Ricci won with Peterborough in '89-'90. Jason Allison won in '93-'94, and the next year Vitali Yachmenev became the first non-North American to win. Future Leafs prospects Alyn McCauley (Ottawa, '96-'97), Brad Boyes (Erie, 2000-01 and '01-'02), and Kyle Wellwood (Belleville, 2002—03) also won.

TODAY

The Hanley Trophy is part of the Hockey Hall of Fame's ever expanding junior trophy case that is becoming as full as the NHL's. The Hall's reputation has ensured that evermore the OHL and CHL are desirous to have their trophies on permanent display at the Hall, to celebrate the game at the junior level and to ensure those young men honoured receive their due recognition.

(left) Rear view of the trophy; (above) two silver shields from the base.

This trophy, made entirely from wood, is remarkably lifelike and pays close attention to exactness. The facial details, the hand holding the hockey stick, the tie, lapels and buttons on his jacket all give Hanley a distinguished appearance fitting to his contributions to the game.

1976 CANADA CUP

1976

THE NAME

Coined by tournament organizer Alan Eagleson, the name of this trophy reflects the origin and location of the first truly international hockey series ever played between the world's top hockey nations.

THE TROPHY

Weighing in at 95 lbs., this is far and away the heaviest hockey trophy. Made of a silver alloy and augmented by a base bearing the name, it was designed and crafted for the first Canada Cup tournament in 1976. It was used again in 1981, when the Soviet Union defeated Canada, and after the victory the winning team tried to steal the Cup home. However, Alan Eagleson and Hockey Hall of Fame curator Lefty Reid caught up with the Soviet team at the airport, and as the players ran through the terminal with their very heavy booty, they dropped it, thus the dent in the tip of the highest point! After this incident, a second Canada Cup trophy was made to ensure any theft in the future would not compromise the original design. The new version weighed about a third the original.

GENESIS

The Canada Cup tournaments would never have occurred but for the extraordinary success of the Summit Series 1972 in which Paul Henderson saved the day for Canada in game eight at Luzhniki Arena in Moscow on September 28, 1972. That climactic battle was borne of Canada's frustration at the World Championships where every year their amateurs (university students, juniors, and the like) played "amateurs" from the Soviet Union, men in their twenties and thirties who trained eleven months of the year for many years specifically for the World Championships and Olympics. The Summit Series was the first chance to pit the best players from each nation, amateur or professional, against each other. The Canada Cup took that one step further, inviting the top six hockey nations in the world to send their very best players to a round robin tournament.

FIRST WINNER

Canada won the first Canada Cup at the Montreal Forum on September 15, 1976, in dramatic fashion. The Canadians had gone through the round robin by winning four of five games, losing only a 1-0 decision to Czechoslovakia, whom they met in the best-of-three finals. In game one of that series, Canada slaughtered the visitors 6-0, but game two was far from a walkover. Canada led 2-0 after the first but by early in the third the Czechs had tied the score. Bobby Clarke put the Canadians ahead, but then their opponents scored twice to take a 5-4 lead, the fifth goal coming from Marian Stastny at 16:00. Less than a minute later, though, the Philadelphia Line of Clarke, Bill Barber, and Reg Leach tied the game, Barber converting a Leach pass. In the overtime, Sittler scored one of the most memorable goals in Canadian international hockey history, skating down the left wing, faking a slapshot to draw Czech goalie Vladimir Dzurilla out of the goal, and sliding the puck into the vacated net.

CHAMPIONS' HISTORY

Canada has been in every Canada Cup/World Cup finals ever played, but in 1981, the second of the Canada Cups, the team suffered a humiliating loss to the Soviets, 8-1 in Montreal, thanks to the spectacular goaltending of Vladislav Tretiak and the less-than-stellar play of Mike Liut in the Canadian net. In 1984, Canada beat Sweden 2-0 in the best-of-three and in 1987 it was a three-game classic over the Soviets, all games being decided by a 6-5 score. In 1991, Canada beat the U.S. in two straight games, but in the 1996 rematch (now called the World Cup), it was the Americans that prevailed in three games. In 2004, Canada was back on top, beating Finland in a one-game finals, 3-2 at Air Canada Centre, Toronto.

TODAY

The Canada Cup trophy passed quietly out of circulation with the end of the Eagleson era. It gave way to a new World Cup of Hockey trophy, and the Hockey Hall of Fame now possesses all Canada Cup trophies. The spirit of the original trophy remains, however, as best-on-best tournaments have become the standard by which all great hockey is judged, be it NHL players at the Olympics or World Cup competitions.

Detail of the trophy's bilingual base from a term coined by Alan Eagleson.

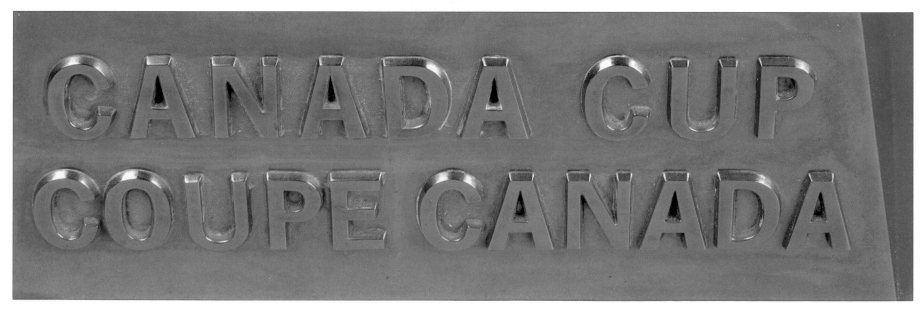

Weighing some 95 lbs., this first version of the Canada Cup was a mighty lift for members of Team Canada after their 6-5 victory over Czechoslovakia at Maple Leaf Gardens to claim the prize in the first ever international tournament featuring "best on best" among many nations.

FRANK J. SELKE TROPHY

1977-PRESENT

THE NAME

Frank Selke began his NHL executive career as an assistant to Conn Smythe in Toronto but left in 1946 to run the Montreal Canadiens. It was under his guidance that the Habs won six Stanley Cups in one remarkable eight-year stretch (1952-60).

THE TROPHY

Most of hockey's bowl-shaped trophies in the tradition of the Stanley Cup give the appearance of doubling as a vessel for champagne and other celebratory beverages, but the Selke, with its undulating lip, offers no such possibility. Instead, it is purely an ornamental, sterling silver trophy with ribbons streamed together along the side of the bowl and ringed handles on two sides held in the jaws of lions. The wood base is hexagonal, each side allowing for six silver plaques, in the shape of pucks, with winners' names.

GENESIS

The NHL's Board of Governors introduced this trophy in November 1977 to honour one of the greatest builders of the game at the professional level and did so by creating an award for the best defensive forward in the league.

FIRST WINNER

This was a trophy created almost exclusively for Bob Gainey of the Canadiens, for it was Gainey's superb all-'round play that drew attention to the very definition of defensive forward. Gainey was a terrific skater and perfectly capable scorer, but he proved so adept at checking another team's top line that his defensive work over-shadowed any touch he had around the opposition goal. He gained his greatest recognition thanks to Soviet coach Anatoli Tarasov who, during the 1976 Canada Cup, called him "technically the best player in the world," meaning he was equally capable defensively as offensively.

CHAMPIONS' HISTORY

Gainey won the Selke Trophy for the first four years of its existence (1977-81) and finished runner-up in 1981-82 when Boston's Steve Kasper won it. It is a trophy that has changed in value over the years. In the late '70s, veterans from the Original Six pointed out that in their day every forward had to be defensively sound! But through the next twenty years, when offense took hold of the NHL game, those skills were often left behind by the great scoring stars such as Wayne Gretzky, Mario Lemieux, and Steve Yzerman. By the mid-1990s, though, defensive hockey and "system" hockey were in vogue, and virtually every forward not only played defensively well but practiced playing the trap as much as working on their wrist shot. Rare is the time that a top scorer has won the Selke Trophy, an exception being 1992-93 when Toronto's Doug Gilmour, with 127 points, won it in what many fans viewed as a consolation prize for the Hart Trophy that year. Guy Carbonneau, another Montreal player who finished his career in Dallas, was, in many ways, the inheritor of Gainey's reputation as a player so skilled at checking the other team's best player that his own scoring skills were undervalued. He won the Selke Trophy three times (1987-89, 1991-92) and played on three Stanley Cup winning teams, but he also scored more than 20 goals in a season on five occasions.

TODAY

There are more candidates these years in the NHL than every before for the Selke as the trap has ruled the game and stifled offence. Kris Draper of Detroit won it in 2003-04, but his ever-present linemate Kirk Maltby might also have won it, along with a dozen or more superb defensive forwards from around the league. Draper and Maltby have been checking and killing penalties together in Detroit since 1996, winning three Stanley Cup championships along the way. They also helped Canada win gold at the 2003 World Championship in Finland.

(left) The base of the bowl; (above) detail of the ornate handles; (right) unique puck-shaped medallions for each year's winner.

One of the newer NHL trophies, the Selke immediately took its rightful place in the NHL's collection of silverware because it honoured both defensive and offensive skill at the same time. In recent years, there have been more potential winners of this than just about any other league award.

ABBY HOFFMAN CUP

1981-PRESENT

THE NAME

In 1955, an eight-year-old girl named Abigail Hoffman wanted to play hockey, but much to her surprise she discovered there were no existing girls' teams for which she could sign up. So, Abigail cut her hair short and registered for a boys' hockey team in Toronto. She also shortened her name to the more masculine "Ab," and became a star player on her team. Before the season was over, however, her secret was out and the next year she entered a girls' league. Hoffman went on to represent Canada at the Olympics in middle-distance track, specializing in the 880-yard run. In all, she represented Canada at four Olympics, culminating in 1976 when she became the first female flag bearer for the country at the opening ceremonies. She also competed in numerous Commonwealth and Pan-Am Games as well.

THE TROPHY

The least ornamental and simplest trophy in the collection, the Abby Hoffman Cup features a plain bowl sitting on a two-tiered wood base. The base accommodates the most rudimentary plaques with the year and team name of each victory, and the bowl has not a word or decorative element save for a perforated rim.

GENESIS

In 1981, Hoffman and Maureen McTeer helped spearhead efforts to organize women's hockey on a national scale with the goal to hold a Canadian championship for women. It was the first time that the best teams from across the country played at one championship.

FIRST WINNER

The Agincourt Canadians, representing Ontario, were the first winners of the Abby Hoffman Cup in 1982, defeating the Edmonton Chimos in Brantford, Ontario.

CHAMPIONS' HISTORY

In the early days, it was the Hamilton Golden Hawks and Edmonton Chimos that dominated, each winning back-to-back championships. Sherbrooke won three in a row (1988-90), and only Team Quebec (1994-96) has been able to replicate that feat. Ontario has won the trophy nine times, Quebec eight.

TODAY

The Abby Hoffman Cup endures to this day and is more alive than ever. In 1999, the National Women's Hockey League was created, a more sophisticated and representative league than the Central Ontario Women's Hockey League, which began in 1992. The Hoffman Cup is now accompanied by other significant trophies from this championship: the Fran Rider Cup is given to the second-place team; the Maureen McTeer Trophy for third place; the Mickey Walker Award for most sportsmanlike player; and, the Isobel Gathorne Hardy Award for contribution to women's hockey are all awarded annually. The trophy is competed for by a combination of provincial champions and provincial teams put together specifically for the tournament in areas where league play doesn't exist or is not of the highest quality possible.

(left) The shield honouring Calgary's 2002-03 championship; (top) other winners from the trophy's wood base; (below) the plate dedicating the trophy.

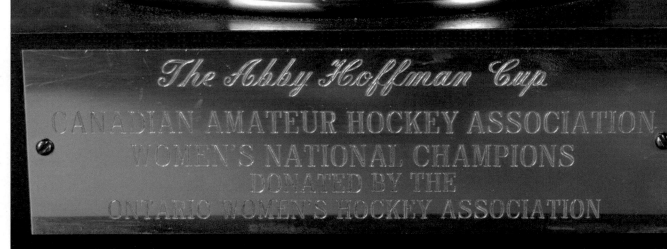

One of the simplest-looking trophies in the collection, the Abby Hoffman Cup is nonetheless vital to women's hockey in Canada where more women play the game than anywhere else in the world. That it is named for Hoffman, a pioneer in hockey, is fittingly appropriate.

HOBEY BAKER MEMORIAL AWARD TROPHY

1980-PRESENT

THE NAME

Hobey Baker was famous at Princeton University for both hockey and football at the turn of the 20th century. In 1914, he enlisted with the Lafayette Escadrille as a pilot in World War I, and shortly before he was to return home he perished in an accident while testing a repaired plane.

THE TROPHY

Deceptively heavy, this two-piece trophy consists of a plastic, glass base with an inscription on the front and a sculpture of a hockey player coming to a sliding stop on top. The glass is durable but very heavy and the sculpture sits on top without adhesion.

GENESIS

The Decathlon Athletic Club in Bloomington, Minnesota sponsored this trophy on the suggestion of its chief executive officer, Chuck Bard, who came up with the idea out of his desire to create something for hockey commensurate to college basketball's Wooden Award. In 1980, Bard hired local artist Bill Mack to sculpt an appropriate trophy for the player adjudged to be the finest in NCAA play annually. Mack used Steve Christoff as a model, photographing him in more than 50 typical hockey poses before deciding on the final version of a skater stopping quickly and spraying ice. Christoff was a member of the USA's Miracle on Ice team that won gold at the 1980 Olympic Winter Games in Lake Placid, New York that February.

FIRST WINNER

Centre Neal Broten of the University of Minnesota won the first Hobey Baker in 1980-81. Like Christoff, he had played on the Miracle on Ice gold medal team, and in the 1980-81 season averaged nearly two points a game for the Bulldogs.

CHAMPIONS' HISTORY

While this is an award strictly for American colleges, the scholarship system in the U.S. has meant that many Canadians have been recruited for NCAA play and as a result almost as many players north of the 49th parallel have won the Hobey Baker as native Americans. George McPhee was the first Canadian to win, in 1982, and in 2004 Junior Lessard of Quebec won while attending the University of Minnesota-Duluth. To its credit, the Hobey Baker has generally been awarded to players who move on to the NHL. Lane MacDonald, son of longtime NHLer Parker MacDonald is a rare exception. He was awarded the Hobey Baker in 1989, but a series of serious head injuries prevented him from playing pro in North America. Interestingly, only two goalies have ever won: Robb Stauber (University of Minnesota) in 1988 and Ryan Miller (Michigan State) in 2001. Only one non-North American has ever won. In 2003, Peter Sejna, a native of the Czech Republic playing for Colorado College, was deemed the best college player over runners-up that included David LeNeveu, Zach Parise, and John-Michael Liles. No player has ever won the trophy twice, and only twice has the same university won it in consecutive years. Tom Kurvers in 1984 and Bill Watson the next year, both of the University of Minnesota-Duluth won, as did Scott Pellerin (1992) and Paul Kariya ('93) win it for University of Maine.

TODAY

The model of the trophy that resides in the Hockey Hall of Fame is a replica of the original, created by the Decathlon Club especially for the Hall. Each player receives a miniature version of this trophy, and the Decathlon Club keeps the original in Bloomington. The winner for 2004-05, in the trophy's 25th season, was forward Marty Sertich of Colorado College. Sertich was a linemate of Sejna the previous year and led the Tigers to the WCHA championship in '04-'05.

Detail of the stick and mid-section of the trophy with acknowledgement to the club that initiated the award.

HOBEY BAKER MEMORIAL AWARD
PRESENTED ANNUALLY TO THE OUTSTANDING COLLEGIATE HOCKEY PLAYER
IN THE UNITED STATES BY THE
DECATHLON ATHLETIC CLUB OF BLOOMINGTON, MINNESOTA

Modelled on Steve Christoff, a member of USA's Miracle on Ice team from the 1980 Olympics, the Hobey Baker honours the first great American hockey player. Although Baker perished before the NHL began, his legacy lived on through his play on ice and meritorious conduct off it.

WILLIAM M. JENNINGS TROPHY

1981-PRESENT

THE NAME

For many years a governor and president of the New York Rangers, William Jennings devoted much of his life to developing hockey in the United States.

THE TROPHY

On the one hand a simple trophy, on the other inventive, the Jennings is a goalies-only award started in 1981-82. It has three tiers of wood, and the names of the winners are engraved on small goalie sticks nailed to the sides of this base. The year sits along the blade of the small silver stick while the name(s) appear on the shaft. The bowl on top is perfectly round and without adornment save an image of a goalie in relief in traditional pose.

GENESIS

When the Jennings Trophy was introduced for the 1981-82 season, it necessarily marked a major redefinition of the Vezina Trophy. The NHL's board of governors created the Jennings for the goalie or goalies who allowed the fewest goals during the season with a minimum of 25 games played, criteria that virtually replicated the Vezina's. As a result, the Vezina became an MVP trophy for goalies that was awarded by vote.

FIRST WINNER

Rick Wamsley and Denis Herron in Montreal led the NHL by allowing a mere 223 goals in the 80-game schedule in '81-'82, a whopping 27 goals better than the second ranked Islanders. It was the first and last Jennings victory for both goalies. Wamsley had a sensational 23-7-7 record and 2.75 goals-against average in 38 games played while Herron was 12-6-8 and a 2.64 GAA in 27 games. Richard Sevigny appeared in just 17 games for the Habs this year, below the required number, and didn't get his name on the Jennings. Oddly, the team lost in the first round of the playoffs, eliminated by Quebec in a fierce best-of-five series three games to two.

CHAMPIONS' HISTORY

Like the Art Ross and Rocket Richard trophies, the Jennings is a statistical award rather than one decided by vote. The occasional obscure goalie has his name on the

Jennings, but it is also very much a precursor to hall of fame glory. Patrick Roy won it four times with Montreal and a fifth time with Colorado, and Martin Brodeur a like number with New Jersey. Grant Fuhr, Ed Belfour, and Dominik Hasek have also won it, but so, too, have Roland Melanson (with Billy Smith and the Islanders in '82-'83) and Darren Jensen (with Bob Froese in Philadelphia in '85-'86). Because of the nature of the goalies' position, the Jennings is more often a shared trophy between a starting goalie and his backup. Only nine times has one goalie won the award outright, and more amazing is that three of those

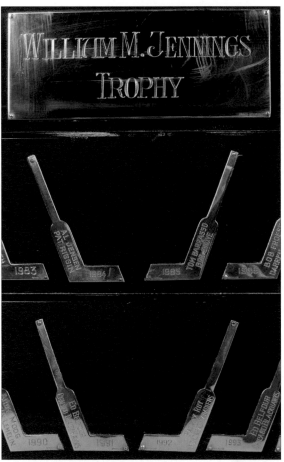

times that goalie was Ed Belfour with Chicago (in 1990-91, 1992-93, 1994-95). Only once have players from two teams shared the award. In 2002-03, Brodeur shared the Jennings with two Flyers' goalies, Roman Cechmanek and Robert Esche. Only Belfour and Roy have won the Jennings with two teams during their careers.

TODAY

The Vezina is one of the original and oldest NHL awards, but like so much else about the game, the trophy has endured as the game has changed. Today, the Vezina honours the best

goalie by vote, and the modern William Jennings is given based on the more statistical goals-against average leaders. Martin Brodeur won the Jennings in 2003-04 with a GAA of 2.03 in 75 games. He also led the league in wins (38) and shutouts (11), and the Devils allowed just 164 goals in 82 games. Because Brodeur played so much, the team's other two goalies, Corey Schwab and Scott Clemmensen, played a mere three and four games, respectively, and their names do not appear on the award.

(left) Goal-stick-shaped plaques honour the winners; (below) the goalie as he appears on the side of the bowl; (bottom) another selection of winning names from the early 1980s.

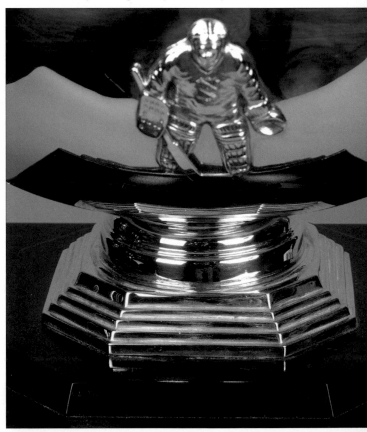

When the Jennings Trophy was introduced in 1981, it not only replaced the Vezina Trophy it also served to give goalies two awards specifically for them, one based on statistics (the Jennings), the other on vote (the Vezina, for best goalie in the NHL).

PRESIDENTS' TROPHY

1985-PRESENT

THE NAME

Continuing in a long line of predecessors, the Presidents' Trophy was donated by the NHL's Board of Governors in 1985.

THE TROPHY

The triangular Presidents' Trophy features a shallow and wide glass bowl on top held by three crossed hockey sticks. These sticks sit on a triangular base. Beneath it are three metal columns about a foot and a half high supported by a thicker triangle base made primarily of wood. Silver plaques on the three sides of the wood base identify the trophy and list the winning teams.

GENESIS

First there was the O'Brien Trophy, symbolic of first place at the end of the regular season. Then there was the O'Brien for the Canadian Division winners and the Prince of Wales for the American Division winners. But after years without a trophy for the top team after the grueling regular season, the NHL decided to introduce a new trophy, thoroughly modern, for the top team in terms of points after the regular season (in the case of a tie, most victories would decide the winner). This team trophy also carries with it a hefty cheque for $350,000, to be distributed by the team among its players and staff as it saw fit. Interestingly, there has been a jinx factor attached to its winning, the top regular season team rarely carrying forward to produce a Cup-winning season as well.

FIRST WINNER

The Presidents'-Stanley Cup jinx began during the first year in existence of the Presidents' Trophy, won by the overpowering Edmonton Oilers at the end of the '85-'86 season. Destined to win their third straight Cup, they were eliminated by Calgary on a flukey own goal by Steve Smith who banked the puck in off goalie Grant Fuhr while trying to make a pass. The Oilers erased the curse the next year, capturing both the Presidents' Trophy and the more prestigious Stanley Cup.

CHAMPIONS' HISTORY

It's the trophy nobody consciously wants to win or tries to win, but it is important nonetheless. Edmonton in 1987, Calgary in 1989, the Rangers in 1994, Dallas in 1999, Colorado in 2001, and Detroit in 2002 are the only teams to win the Stanley Cup the same year they won the Presidents' Trophy. It's not so much a jinx as it is a strategic fact that a team that places first overall after an 82-game season has probably exerted too much of its energy and not saved enough for the more grueling four rounds of best-of-seven playoffs. Ironically, every team that has won the Stanley Cup has just previously won the Presidents' Trophy, but not necessarily in the same season. The league gives the winning of the trophy some extra incentive, though, by awarding the Presidents' Trophy winner home-ice advantage in every round of the playoffs. This came into play in 1987, when the Oilers won at home in game seven. The Rangers in 1994 and Colorado in 2001 also won at home in the seventh and deciding game of a Cup finals thanks to their first overall rank at the end of the regular season.

TODAY

The Detroit Red Wings won 48 games in 2003-04, tops in the league, and finished with 109 total points, three ahead of Tampa Bay, to win the Presidents' Trophy. But when the Wings were eliminated by Calgary in the Western Conference semi-finals, the Lightning became the top team remaining and assumed home-ice advantage for every series they played, winning the Cup in game seven games, at home, against those same Flames.

(left) A detail of the crossed sticks that support the glass bowl at the top of the trophy; (above) descriptive plaque at the base of the trophy.

NATIONAL HOCKEY LEAGUE
PRESIDENTS' TROPHY

Sleek, modern, inventive, the Presidents' Trophy has a triangular presentation similar to the Lester B. Pearson Award. The two are made of radically different materials, however, and this mostly glass and metal award is a distinct example of a modern NHL honour.

JACK RILEY CUP

THE NAME

Jack Riley's life in hockey extended the full span of his adult life. As a player, he appeared with Detroit, Montreal, and Boston in the NHL during the 1930s before embarking on a lengthy minor-league career that took him mostly through the AHA. He played one game with the Red Wings in 1932-33 and for two years after established himself as a full-time forward with the Canadiens. A trade to Boston more or less ended his time in the NHL. After retiring as a skater in 1945, Riley became a general manager until 1964 when he was named president of the AHL, a position he held for three years. He then became a pro scout with the expansion Pittsburgh Penguins franchise, but in 1975 he accepted a new challenge when he took the job as commissioner of the Southern Hockey League.

THE TROPHY

The Jack Riley Cup calls to mind an amalgamation of several trophies in the Hockey Hall of Fame's collection. The two-tiered wood base is a common design element which allows for size and shape, providing room to display plaques with the trophy's name and the annual winners. The four hockey players on top of the first tier, which is bigger than the second tier, recall the Shipstads and Johnson Trophy. The plain silver bowl on top, without any identifying features, is similar to the cup that crowns the Jack Adams Award. Regardless, the Riley Cup consists of only eight winning teams, so the lowest base has a plaque on only one of its four sides.

GENESIS

When the new East Coast Hockey League started up in 1988, it decided to honour a man who had spent his life in the minors by naming its championship trophy after Riley.

FIRST WINNER

The ECHL got off on the right foot when it provided fans with a wild and unpredictable playoffs in its first year of operation. The five-team league eliminated only one team during the regular season (Virginia), and in round one of the post-season first place Erie Panthers played fourth place Carolina Thunderbirds. Despite finishing 22 points behind the Panthers, the Thunderbirds swept Erie aside in four straight games to play Johnstown, which had dispatched Knoxville with equal ease. The Chiefs humiliated Carolina in the first two games of the Riley Cup finals by scores of 8-1 and 6-1, but the Thunderbirds rallied for a 7-4 win in game three. Game four in Carolina was postponed because the ice was bad, but Carolina still won the fourth game, in Johnstown, to even the series. They in turn hammered the Chiefs 7-1 to take a 3-2 lead in the finals, but the Chiefs forced game seven with a 7-4 win in Carolina. In the final game of the season, on the road, Carolina, the lowest of the playoff teams, won the first Riley Cup with a 7-4 victory over the Chiefs.

CHAMPIONS' HISTORY

The Hampton Road Admirals (1990-92) and Toledo Storm (1992-94) are the only ECHL teams to win consecutive championships. In '90-'91, the Admirals featured future great goalie Olaf Kolzig who had been drafted by

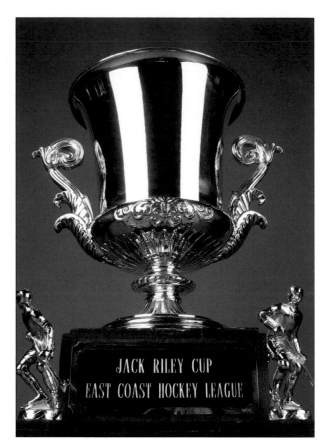

Washington two years earlier but who had yet to make an impression at the NHL level. The next year, the Admirals won the Cup in a four-game sweep of Louisville, their dominance not in question even though they didn't have one scorer in the league's top ten. The Storm were much the same. Not a team with even one dominant player, it was nevertheless a dominating team. In 1992-93, they beat Wheeling in double overtime of game six to win their first Riley Cup, and the next year, again without a top-ten scorer, they beat Raleigh in five games (the first two games of the series in overtime).

TODAY

The ECHL retired the Riley Cup in 1996 and re-named its championship trophy in honour of its one and only commissioner, Pat Kelly. The Kelly Cup was a newly-created trophy, and the Riley Cup was sent to the Hockey Hall of Fame where it continues to represent a man and a league that found its place on a crowded hockey map.

(left) Detail of one corner of the trophy; (above) a low-angle view of the trophy.

JACK RILEY CUP
EAST COAST HOCKEY LEAGUE

1988-89	CAROLINA THUNDERBIRDS
1989-90	GREENSBORO MONARCHS
1990-91	HAMPTON ROADS ADMIRALS
1991-92	HAMPTON ROADS ADMIRALS
1992-93	TOLEDO STORM
1993-94	TOLEDO STORM
1994-95	RICHMOND RENEGADES
1995-96	CHARLOTTE CHECKERS

The short history of the Riley Cup is nonetheless an important part in the long history of the game. It connects a man who played in the 1930s (Riley) to a modern league that thrived as hockey continued its expansion in the United States to places no one in Riley's time could have envisaged.

FRANK "KING" CLANCY MEMORIAL TROPHY

THE NAME

No man in hockey did as much for the game and for as long as did King Clancy. His NHL career began as a player with Ottawa in 1921. He later became a coach after retiring in 1937, then an NHL referee for more than a decade, after which began an affiliation with the Leafs that lasted until his death in 1986.

THE TROPHY

The inscription on the top of the lid of this trophy is curious, to say the least: "This Cup was given by King George the third to his Godson George John West Viscount Cantilupe, born October 26th, 1791." The sides of the cup portray two coats of arms, betraying the fact that this was anything but a hockey trophy when it was created. Harold Ballard, the Leafs' owner who donated the trophy, bought this cup from an unknown source. But, by virtue of its date, it is by far the oldest hockey trophy in existence! The round, two-tiered wood base, not much greater in circumference than the base of the bowl, is slim and contains the winners' names on silver shields.

GENESIS

Shaken to the core by his best friend's death, Leafs' owner Harold Ballard proposed to the NHL's Board of Governors in 1988 that a trophy in Clancy's name be presented every year to a player who had made particularly important contributions to his community, notably in charitable work with the less fortunate.

FIRST WINNER

There was little doubt who the first winner of the Clancy Trophy would be, for no one was influenced by and admired Clancy more than Lanny McDonald. He came to the Leafs in the early 1970s, a scared Prairie boy trying to make it in the NHL in the hockey capital, and Clancy took McDonald under his wing and helped him become a star in the league. McDonald combined his skills on the ice with charitable efforts off it that made him among the most popular athletes in Toronto's history. His frequent visits to hospitals were important parts of his schedule, but his work with the Special Olympics made him a greater man than any goal or pass could ever hope to do.

CHAMPIONS' HISTORY

No player has ever won the Clancy Trophy twice, and it is to hockey's credit that this is so. More than any other sport, the players and the city they play in are intertwined. Hockey players are more generous with their time than other athletes and see the importance of being a role model to kids, largely because they, too, had idols growing up and they know the importance just a few hours' effort is to any group or organization. Winners of the Clancy Trophy are not necessarily the most skilled players in the game, although Bryan Trottier and Ray Bourque have also won the Clancy Trophy during a Hall of Fame career. But players such as Kris King, a fourth-liner during his career, and Rob Ray, a fighter in anyone's books, have made tremendous impact on their communities through their work off ice with kids who won't ever know the luxuries these players enjoyed every day of their careers. The Clancy Trophy might have little to do with on-ice ability, but it is as important as any the league awards annually to its players.

TODAY

The 2004 Clancy Trophy was given to Jarome Iginla, and the league is the better for it. Iginla is the perfect combination of superstar player and modest member of society both. In 2002, he signed a lucrative contract with Calgary, although he could have signed for more money with a richer team. He has won the Richard Trophy twice and a gold medal with Canada at the 2002 Olympics. But as important, he always wears a smile, betraying his knowledge of being blessed with skill. His work both during the hockey year and in the off season in Calgary have made him immensely popular in that city, and he is a truly amazing human being even if he never plays another NHL game.

(above left) Detail of the original dedication of this trophy from 1791; (above) the trophy with its lid removed; (near left) the modern dedication indicating the trophy's hockey significance.

If this trophy looks majestic and classic, not modern and innovative, it's because this silver was crafted in 1791. Leafs owner Harold Ballard bought it and converted it into the contemporary Clancy Trophy!

1988 WORLD JUNIOR CHAMPIONSHIP TROPHY

1988

THE NAME

This trophy simply bears the name of the tournament designated by the IIHF to determine the best under-20 team in world competition.

THE TROPHY

Cast in bronze with gold-painted lettering, this heavy plaque was of a standard type for the IIHF for a few years before giving way to a more traditional trophy. Each champion team for each tournament received a similar plaque which the member federation got to keep and display as it saw fit.

GENESIS

The 1970s were a time of massive change in international hockey. In 1970, Canada withdrew from all competition because it was not allowed to use any professional players against the pros of Iron Curtain countries. This, in turn, led to the '72 Summit Series, the first ever true best-on-best tournament. Out of this came the 1976 Canada Cup and the return to the World Championship by Canada in 1977

which was now allowed to use pros. As a result, there was no place for Canada's best young players to play. The IIHF filled the breach in '77 by creating a world tournament for under-20 players. The World Junior Championship had started as an invitational in 1974, but three years later the time was right to make this an annual, IIHF-sanctioned event. It has since become the premier junior tournament in Canada every year, whether the country hosts the WJC or watches on TSN, the network that has supported the tournament with unparalleled devotion.

FIRST WINNER

This 1988 Canadian team featured a mix of future great NHLers and junior stars who never experienced anywhere near the success as this gold medal. The tournament was also played on a backdrop of redemption and anger fuelled by Canada's disqualification from the WJC the previous year when the team had a great chance to win gold but was induced into a bench-clearing brawl by the Soviets that caused both nations to be removed from competition. The brawl in Piestany, Czechoslovakia, was difficult to stomach for the players, but they vowed to win their deserved gold the next year. Led by team captain Theo Fleury, they did just that, going undefeated in seven games and winning gold right in the Soviet Union. This was a mature Team Canada featuring eleven 19-year-olds and just one 17-year-old (Trevor Linden). Every player on the team was drafted

into the NHL, and all but two played in that league (the exceptions being Marc Laniel and Scott McCrady). Canada and the Soviet Union met on New Year's Day, 1988 in what amounted to a gold medal game. Canada had won three and tied one in their first four games, and the Soviets were 4-0 to start, so clearly the winner of this game had control the rest of the way. There was to be no brawl this day; in fact, there were but nine, harmless minor penalties called all night. Canada built a 2-0 lead after the first period on goals by Fleury and Linden, and in the second the Soviets closed the gap, 2-1, before Laniel restored the two-goal advantage. Laniel and Valeri Zelepukin each scored, and after a goalless third period Canada emerged 3-2 winners, goalie Jimmy Waite stopping 38 of the 40 shots he faced (by contrast, Canada had just 16 shots on Alexei Sheblanov). The Canadians then hammered West Germany 8-1 and Poland 9-1 to win a gold they had been denied a year earlier by the Soviets.

CHAMPIONS' HISTORY

Of the 29 World Junior tournaments that have been played, the Soviets/Russia (12) and Canada (11) have accounted for 23 gold medals. Only Finland (1987, 1998) and the Czechs (2000, 2001) have won more than once. The USA won in 2004 and Sweden in 1981.

TODAY

The World Junior Championship has grown in importance and remains the key tournament for junior-aged players every year. The tournament enjoys a particularly significant reputation in Canada, where attendance records are broken virtually every time the country hosts the event. Elsewhere, while the competition remains of the highest calibre, fan support is far less impressive. Canada won gold in January 2005 for the first time since 1997, going undefeated and earning recognition as perhaps the best junior team of all time. In 2005, the IIHF awarded Canada a special privilege never bestowed upon another country. It announced that Canada would host the World Junior Championship every three years in recognition of the special support that tournament enjoys in the motherland of the game. Canada had already been granted the 2006 tournament, in Vancouver, and it will now also be guaranteed to host again in 2009 and 2012, after which the IIHF will re-assess the success of this strategy.

Detail of the plaque given specifically for this year's winning nation.

A heavy, bronze dish, this design was used by the IIHF for a number of years for the World Junior Championships and Women's World Championships, a new one being made every year to honour the champion instead of the Canadian practice of using the same trophy year after year.

BRABHAM CUP

THE NAME

Henry Brabham, along with Bill Coffey, was a founder of the East Coach Hockey League (ECHL). Brabham was a former mayor of Vinton, Virginia, and later owned the Salem Raiders hockey team. He was enthusiastically involved in hockey in Virginia for more than 20 years, and it was his idea to start a league that had merit as a developmental league and not just a beer league with brawls every night. He named friend and longtime coach Pat Kelly the league's first commissioner, and Kelly spent eight years growing the league and enhancing its reputation.

THE TROPHY

One of the simplest trophies on display, the Brabham Cup has a wood base that is nearly double the size of the bowl it supports. And, because it honoured league champions of the ECHL for only eight years, that base has a plaque for winners on only one side. The bowl sits on a second, smaller block of wood and is itself utterly unpretentious and without a name or mark on it.

GENESIS

The ECHL came out of the defunct All-American Hockey League in which Brabham and Coffey were owners of several teams. Brabham owned the Johnstown Chiefs and Virginia Lancers, and Coffey owned the Carolina Thunderbirds. When this league folded, they started the ECHL with those teams and two new franchises in Knoxville, Tennessee and Erie, Pennsylvania. Brabham owned the Erie Panthers when the ECHL started up, and it was his team, appropriately, that won the first Brabham Cup for finishing first in the standings at the end of the 60-game regular season in 1988-89. When the league went to two divisions, it was the team with the most points that won the Brabham Cup.

FIRST WINNER

Erie finished comfortably ahead of Johnstown to win the first Brabham Cup with a 37-20-3 record. The Panthers' 77 points were seven better than the Chiefs, and they were the only team to score more than 300 goals in the season (327). Ron Hansis coached a team that included nothing but unheralded players who never made it to the NHL, starting with goalies Paul Kenny and Tony Mongillo as well as skaters such as Darryl Moise, Doug Stromback, and Grant Ottenbreit. Still, Daryl Harpe led the ECHL with 122 points and Kenny was second in GAA with a 4.12 average.

CHAMPIONS' HISTORY

During the eight years this trophy was used, no winner of the Brabham Cup went on to win the Riley Cup as playoff champions. Additionally, during these early years of the ECHL, the league was hardly a feeder for the NHL and as such was populated by players whose accomplishments were limited to that league. Len Soccio, for instance, was just beginning what would be a 20-year pro career which saw the

Ontarian play for Germany at the World Championships for years. In 1989-90, he played on the Brabham Cup team in Winston-Salem. Stan Drulia helped the Knoxville Cherokees to the Brabham Cup the following year, and he ended up in the NHL with Tampa Bay in '92-'93 and then, amazingly, made the NHL team full-time seven years later after spending all the interim time in the IHL. Teams from Toledo, Wheeling, and Richmond also won this first incarnation of the Brabham Cup.

TODAY

In 1996, the ECHL retained the name of the Brabham Cup and ensured it was awarded annually for league champions of the regular season, a new trophy was crafted and the original retired to the Hockey Hall of Fame. The Riley Cup, meanwhile, was retired in 1996 and replaced by the Kelly Cup, the league deciding that it was time to honour Pat Kelly, the commissioner, for all his work in making the ECHL a respectable league and a first-rate business.

EAST COAST HOCKEY LEAGUE LEAGUE CHAMPIONS

HENRY BRABHAM IV

1988 – 1989	ERIE PANTHERS	
1989 – 1990	WINSTON-SALEM THUNDERBIRDS	
1990 – 1991	KNOXVILLE CHEROKEES	
1991 – 1992	TOLEDO STORM	
1992 – 1993	WHEELING THUNDERBIRDS	
1993 – 1994	KNOXVILLE CHEROKEES	
1994 – 1995	WHEELING THUNERBIRDS	
1995 – 1996	RICHMOND RENEGADES	

(left) A bird's eye view of the trophy; (above) detail of the plaque honouring winning teams.

EAST COAST HOCKEY LEAGUE
LEAGUE CHAMPIONS

HENRY BRABHAM IV

1988 – 1989 ERIE PANTHERS
1989 – 1990 WINSTON-SALEM THUNDERBIRDS
1990 – 1991 KNOXVILLE CHEROKEES
1991 – 1992 TOLEDO STORM
1992 – 1993 WHEELING THUNDERBIRDS
1993 – 1994 KNOXVILLE CHEROKEES
1994 – 1995 WHEELING THUNERBIRDS
1995 – 1996 RICHMOND RENEGADES

The Brabham Cup is sister trophy to the Jack Riley Cup, the former honouring regular-season champions, the latter for playoff winners. The Riley has since given way to the Kelly Cup, but the Brabham remains in circulation though with a new design. This original rests in the Hockey Hall of Fame.

1990 WOMEN'S WORLD CHAMPIONSHIP TROPHY

1990

THE NAME

From 1987, when the first unofficial world women's championship took place, to 1990, when the tournament became an annual, fully-sanctioned IIHF event, women's international hockey was played frequently but not consistently. This 1990 tournament was the first time the IIHF, international hockey's governing body, made it part of its program.

THE TROPHY

Like the World Junior trophy for men, this was a simple, round plaque that incorporated the IIHF logo and the tournament name. It was cast with a type of bronze and weighs in excess of 20 lbs.

GENESIS

The 1987 tournament, organized by Fran Rider and played in Ontario, was the first attempt by women to stage a world tournament. That it took place was a success in itself, and participating teams had to pay their own way, including travel expenses, hotels and food, and participation fees. Over the course of the next three years, Rider and representatives from other leading hockey nations worked to convince the IIHF to make a women's championship an official IIHF event, which it did in 1990.

FIRST WINNER

Eight teams arrived in Ottawa in March 1990 to play in the first Women's World Championship, and as has been the case ever since, it was a Canada-USA finals. European entries included Sweden, Norway, Finland, Switzerland, and West Germany, and a Far East representative from Japan rounded out the eight-nation tournament. In the end, though, the North American countries walloped the competition. Canada beat Sweden, Germany, and Japan by scores of 15-1,

17-0, and 18-0, respectively, and the USA had almost as easy a time in dispatching its opponents. In the gold-medal game, Canada prevailed 5-2. Leading the way was Angela James, who had eleven goals in the five games. Vicky Sunohara was also on that team, and 15 years later she was still playing for Canada at the Women's World Championship in Sweden in April 2005. The USA was led by 18-year-old Cammi Granato in 1990, and she, too, remains part of the USA team.

CHAMPIONS' HISTORY

The women played World Championships in 1990, 1992, 1994, and 1997 leading up to the first-ever appearance of women's hockey at the Olympics, in 1998 in Nagano, Japan. Thereafter, it has been an annual event with the exception of 2003 when the worldwide spread of SARS, notably in China where that tournament was scheduled, forced its cancellation. A 2002 World Championship did not take place because the Olympics in Salt Lake City, when Canada won 3-2, replaced the tournament. In each and every gold-medal game, Canada has played the USA, and every bronze-medal game has featured Finland vs. Sweden (except 2001 when Russia won bronze). Amazingly, Canada won every World Championship gold ever contested until 2005 when USA won 1-0 in a shootout to claim its first gold medal. While the Canada-USA rivalry is exciting and features top-level hockey, players and fans alike are waiting for the European nations to catch up and make the tournament more than just a two-team competition.

TODAY

Like the men, the women now have a single trophy that the IIHF hands out every year. In both cases, it is made from the same design, a wood base supporting a silver half-globe with handles on two sides. The winning teams are engraved on small plaques affixed to the wood base. After the celebrations, the winning team gets a replica of the original while the IIHF takes the real trophy back to its offices in Switzerland.

A detail of the dish won by Team Canada for the first official Women's World Championship.

The same design as that used for the World Junior Championship winner, the traditional bronze dish was minted each year for the winning nation. In 1990, in Ottawa, Team Canada defeated USA 5-2 in the gold-medal game, beginning a World Championship undefeated streak that lasted until 2005.

1991 WORLD CHAMPIONSHIP TROPHY

1991

THE NAME

The World Championship Trophy has been competed for annually since 1930 except in Olympic years when the IIHF considered that tournament to act also as the World Championship. Since 1989, it has been played every year, even in Olympics years when a separate tournament followed the Olympics in the spring.

THE TROPHY

A unique honour for world supremacy, this 1991 World Championship trophy is made of bronze and plated with gold. The trunk consists of four, upturned hockey sticks pointing outward, the blades supporting a gold player who holds a stick in one hand (to represent the sport) and a bouquet of flowers in the other (symbolic of victory).

GENESIS

An annual world championship tournament came out of two separate but related events. The first was the inconsistently-annual European championship which started in 1910 and was held again in every year 1911-14, 1921-23, 1925-27, and 1929. At the same time, international hockey experienced a greater success with the Olympics in 1920, 1924, and 1928 during which time Canada not only asserted its superiority but also helped introduce the game as fast, entertaining, and skilful.

FIRST WINNER

Canada won every major international tournament before World War II with the exception of the 1933 World Championship and the 1936 Olympics when a heavily Canadian-born team from Great Britain beat Canada 2-1 to claim gold.

CHAMPIONS' HISTORY

The 1991 World Championship, in Helsinki and Turku, Finland, was one of the most dramatic in history. The eight teams first played a round robin, the top four moving on to a round robin finals, the bottom four to a relegation round robin. In the preliminary round, the Soviets went undefeated, winning six games and tieing Sweden 5-5 on the last day of the first series of games. It was an ominous sign. In its previous six games, the Soviets had surrendered just eleven goals, but the explosive Swedish offense, led by Mats Sundin, Mats Naslund, and Hakan Loob proved too dangerous for Soviet goalie Andrei Trefilov. The Swedes, meanwhile, also went undefeated, but with an unusual record of just three wins and four ties. In the medal round of round robin play, however, the Swedes were almost perfect. They tied Canada 3-3, then hammered USA, 8-4, to set up a gold-medal game on the final day of the tournament against the Soviets. Both teams had three points in the standings, so whoever won this game would win the gold medal. The score was tied 1-1 going into the third period, but the 20-year-old Sundin scored one of the greatest goals in World Championship history. He burst down the right wing, faked a move to the outside and went inside on Soviet defenceman Slava Fetisov, and made a perfect deke on Trefilov to give Tre Kronor a 2-1 win and a gold medal.

TODAY

This replica 1991 gold trophy of a player celebrating a goal was donated to the Hockey Hall of Fame by the Swedish Ice Hockey Association when the Hall expanded to create a new international zone. At the time, the IIHF gave out a new trophy almost every year to its winners, though more recently it has created, like the Stanley Cup, a single trophy that is presented each year.

Details of the replica World Championship trophy for 1991 won by Sweden.

This elegant World Championship trophy went to Sweden thanks to 20-year-old sensation Mats Sundin who scored a brilliant third-period goal to give his team a 2-1 win over the Soviets in Finland. It was only Tre Kronor's second gold since 1962.

SUNSHINE TROPHY

1992-1995

THE NAME

The Sunshine Trophy is emblematic of superiority in the Sunshine Hockey League which featured four teams in, of course, Florida.

THE TROPHY

One of the least hockey-looking hockey trophies in the collection, the Sunshine Trophy has but three team names engraved on a plaque along one of the narrow sides of the base. Four faux wood columns support a flat table which has four gold hawks on the corners and a gold cup with a hockey player on top in the middle. On the base at the bottom, among the four columns is another gold trophy with a smaller section of faux wood and an Olympian-type man holding high a flame.

GENESIS

Indirectly, hockey fans have Wayne Gretzky to thank for the SHL. After his trade to Los Angeles in 1988, he worked and played to increase interest in the game throughout California and the southern United States, hoping to build a fan base from which the league could expand and the American citizenry embrace the game like never before. During the prime of his career, it worked. The NHL gave teams to Anaheim and San Jose; Winnipeg moved to Phoenix and Minnesota to Dallas; the state of Florida got two new franchises in the Florida Panthers and Tampa Bay Lightning. The offshoot of this was greater interest at the lower levels of minor pro leagues. The AHL expanded, causing the IHL and ECHL to expand. The Colonial League started up, and in 1992 the Sunshine league offered players another option. This was truly the lowest level of pro hockey in North America, a four-team circuit that paid players an un-Gretzky-like $200-$275 a week and boarded players two to a room in two-bedroom apartments.

FIRST WINNER

The SHL was dominated by the West Palm Beach Blaze which won the only three championships contested (1992-95). The league was in trouble from the get-go. It started as a five-team operation—West Palm Beach, Daytona Beach Sun Devils, Jacksonville Bullets, Lakeland Ice Warriors, and St. Petersburg Renegades—but the St. Pete's team didn't last

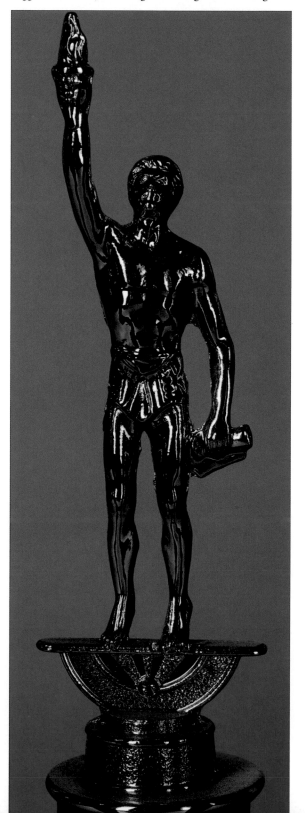

more than a few weeks (20 games, to be exact). West Palm was coached by American-born, former NHLer Bill Nyrop. His lineup was a "who's not" of primarily Canadian talent: Kyle Haviland, Jim Duhart, Rob Celotto, Scott Garro. The biggest name was John Craighead who got into a few games with the Maple Leafs a couple of years later. The Blaze tore through the season winning 38 of 45 games. Second place Jacksonville was 22-23-0 (with two overtime losses), making clear West Palm's superiority. In fact, all teams in the league played a different number of games because of the demise of the Renegades.

CHAMPIONS' HISTORY

In 1993-94, the four teams all played a uniform 54-game schedule and league parity helped stabilize operations. West Palm again finished in first place with a 37-14-0-3 record, but Jacksonville was just eight points behind in the standings. Any inroads the league made through fan support, though, were hampered by excessive fighting and violence on ice, as this account from the West Palm media guide highlights: "The home opener was filled with fights…Many of the fans that brought young children left the auditorium early as a result of the malicious display." In '94-'95, West Palm Beach again led the five-team league (with the addition of the Fresno Falcons) and captured their third successive championship.

TODAY

The SHL did not survive its fourth season and was disbanded for lack of finances and fan interest. The trophy, along with many West Palm Beach Blaze programs and team information, ended up at the Hockey Hall of Fame, where the lowest end of pro hockey remains an integral part of the game's history.

(left) A symbol of victory from the base; (above) detail of the player from the very top of the trophy.

SUNSHINE HOCKEY LEAGUE
CHAMPIONS

Although it lasted for just three years, the Sunshine league was testament to the growing popularity of hockey in the United States, particularly the south. It was undone by lack of fan support, but that was largely due to a lack of big-name players in the league. In the end, the league was a worthy experiment.

1994 WORLD CHAMPIONSHIP TROPHY

1994

THE NAME

The 1994 World Championship represented the 58th tournament in IIHF history, beginning in 1920 with the first Olympics tournament of hockey.

THE TROPHY

Taller than the 1991 version, this 1994 World Championship trophy also is made of bronze and plated with gold. Similarly, the trunk consists of four, upturned hockey sticks pointing outward, the blades supporting a gold player who holds a stick in one hand (to represent the sport) and a bouquet of flowers in the other (symbolic of victory).

WINNER

Canada won one and lost one in 1994, and no doubt everyone in Canada would prefer the results to have been reversed. That is, Canada won gold at the '94 World Championship, in a shootout over Finland, but lost the gold at the '94 Olympics, in a shootout to Sweden. Nonetheless, the World gold was the first for Canada since 1961 when the Trail Smoke Eaters of British Columbia won. The annual poor showing for Canada was a result of never having a chance to send over anything but a makeshift team of non-playoff NHL players (since 1977) and previously of sending university-age players to compete against the best senior men in Europe. The 1994 World Championship took place in

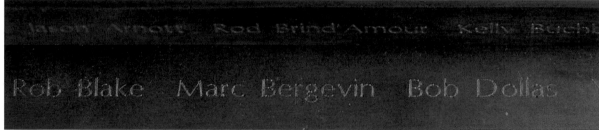

Bolzano, Italy, and Canada fielded one of its strongest teams of recent years. Paul Kariya and Brendan Shanahan were among the forwards; Rob Blake led the defencemen; and, Bill Ranford was in goal. In the first round, Canada had a perfect 5-0-0 record, and in the playoffs the team rounded into form by beating the Czechs 3-2 and the Swedes 6-0 to take one place in the gold medal finals. On the other side, Finland went 4-0-1 in the round robin, and in the playoffs hammered Austria 10-0 and USA 8-0 to earn the other spot in the final game. After three periods of that gold medal showdown, the score was tied 1-1, and ten minutes of overtime failed to decide a winner. The teams headed to a shootout, a format which had haunted Canada a few months earlier when Tommy Salo stopped Paul Kariya after Peter Forsberg had scored for Sweden and gave Tre Kronor Olympic gold. Here was Kariya again, in a shootout, but this time the result was favourable for him. Both teams scored twice in the first five shots, forcing a sudden death shootout, and Luc Robitaille, who had one of those two goals in the first round of the penalty shot competition, scored again to give Canada the victory after Ranford made the final stop. Incredibly, 33 years

had passed since Canada last won gold at the Worlds, but coach Tom Renney took his team to a flawless 8-0-0 run through this tournament for gold.

TODAY

This gold World Championship trophy, taller than the 1991 version of a player celebrating a goal, was made solely for the 1994 winners. As such, it became property of Hockey Canada which in turn donated it to the Hockey Hall of Fame. Previous and subsequent years saw different trophies presented to the winners until 2001 when the IIHF introduced one trophy for annual competition.

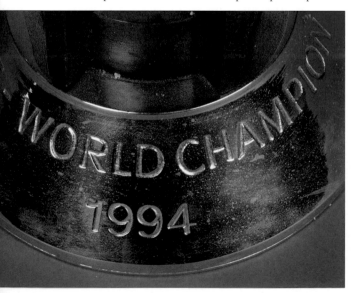

(left) Detail from the base of the trophy; (top, above) the four sticks that support the gold player at the top of the trophy are full with names of the winners, in this case from Canada in 1994.

One of the many World Championship trophies that have been given since the first annual competition in 1930, this was a version that was replicated several times. Canada won the 1994 gold medal (and accompanying trophy), its first victory at the World Championship since 1961.

ROYAL BANK CUP

1995-PRESENT

THE NAME

Like an ever-growing number of trophies, the Royal Bank Cup is named simply after its eponymous sponsor, the Royal Bank.

THE TROPHY

A uniquely designed trophy with a triangular configuration, the Royal Bank Cup has two wood bases that support three pillars in each corner and further support a silver cup on top. The bottom tier is slightly larger than the second one, and both serve to honour the winners whose team names and rosters are engraved on plaques which are attached to the wood. In between the three bronze pillars sits a pointed section of glass. The bowl itself is simple and without inscription of any sort.

GENESIS

The Royal Bank Cup took its name in 1996 as successor to the Centennial Cup, which had started in 1971. Its purpose was to honour the best provincial junior teams in the country in a format that is now similar to the Memorial Cup, which sees regional champions play in a national championship.

FIRST WINNER

The Vernon Vipers defeated the Melfort Mustangs who were in the tournament as the host city. In the five-team, round robin, Melfort went undefeated (4-0-0) while Vernon managed only a 2-2-0 record. Nonetheless, both teams won their semi-finals games and Vernon shut out the hosts 2-0 to win the first Royal Bank Cup. Goals were scored by Dustin Whitecotton and Sjon Wynia. Beau Riedel recorded the shutout.

CHAMPIONS' HISTORY

Amazingly, the level of parity across the country has been the most distinct feature of the Royal Bank Cup. Three winners have come from British Columbia, two from the Maritimes, Alberta, and Saskatchewan, and one from Ontario. In fact, the Vipers are the only team to win twice in the RBC era, their second victory coming in 1999 when they defeated the Charlottetown Abbies in Yorkton, Saskatchewan. The most recent winners were the Weyburn Red Wings which defeated the Camrose Kodiaks at home 3-2 in a final game that was the most dramatic in tournament history. Weyburn led the game 2-0 going into the final period, but Camrose tied the score 2-2 with just 35 seconds left in the game. Undaunted, the Red Wings took the faceoff into enemy territory, and with just 16.6 seconds left in the game Rick Wood jammed a loose puck into the net to give Weyburn a dramatic victory.

TODAY

The Royal Bank Cup is alive and gaining momentum. As the World Junior Championships takes on ever greater meaning during the annual international season, the trickle-down effect has meant greater importance for the Under-18 and Under-17 tournaments, and this in turn has helped the Royal Bank Cup become the second most important trophy for Canadian teenagers to play for nationally after the Memorial Cup.

(left) Detail of the base with winning teams engraved on small plaques; (top) detail of the base of the bowl; (above) a section of glass that rests on the top of the wood base.

In succeeding the Centennial Cup in purpose, the Royal Bank Cup has become an evermore important trophy in junior hockey in Canada. The provincial Junior A ranks are more crowded than the higher-profile Canadian Hockey League, but many of the players who have won the Royal Bank Cup have gone on to great professional success as well.

1996 DEUTSCHLAND CUP

1996

THE NAME

Established in 1987 by the German Ice Hockey Union, the Deutschland Cup was intended to be an annual tournament to promote play among national teams to give Germany's own team playing experience against top nations in the hockey world. Games were played in principal German cities from year to year.

THE TROPHY

Simple and small, this version of the Deutschland Cup was given the Germans after the victory, their second in succession. Sitting on a small marble base, the cup resembles an oversized chalice, ripples in the body leading to the rim and handles on two sides.

FIRST WINNER

The Czechs won in 1987 in a series featuring only Germany and Poland besides themselves.

CHAMPIONS' HISTORY

Held in Stuttgart from November 1-3, this 1996 version of the Deutschland Cup featured Germany, Italy, Canada, and Slovakia. The Germans won for the second straight year, going undefeated. They beat Canada 4-2, Italy 3-1, and Slovakia 4-1 to claim this trophy. Thomas Brandl led the tournament scoring with five points (one goal, four assists). The Germans have won only these two times. Russia/Soviet Union has won four times, the Czech Republic/Czechoslovakia twice, and Canada twice.

The USA won for the first time in 2003 and repeated the next year as winners in a five-team tournament (Canada, Germany, Slovakia, Switzerland, USA).

TODAY

Because this is a short tournament and not a major part of the international hockey calendar, the Deutschland Cup rarely features top players and teams. Instead, visiting countries put together a hodge-podge lineup at the last minute based on player availability and use the few games as an opportunity to give young or inexperienced players the chance to play internationally. The Deutschland Cup might not attract worldwide attention, but it does have its small niche and has established itself in Germany as an elite weekend of hockey for the national team.

Detail of the marble base of the 1996 Deutschland Cup.

EISHOCKEY
DEUTSCHLAND-CUP
1996
1. Platz

DEUTSCHLAND

One of the numerous tournaments during the European hockey season, the Deutschland Cup is competed for by teams from several countries in a round-robin format. It doesn't always attract the biggest names from the various federations, but the international experience players get from the tournament makes it a worthwhile event nonetheless.

1996 WORLD CUP OF HOCKEY TROPHY

1996

THE NAME

Created as a replacement to Alan Eagleson's Canada Cup, the World Cup of Hockey signaled a new era for the sport while continuing to celebrate the game in a format created by Eagleson during his tenure as NHLPA executive director.

THE TROPHY

The World Cup trophy, of course, was no longer the stylized large, silver maple leaf that was the Canada Cup but a new creation altogether. The basis for the new trophy came out of the logo, which features two players facing off, their extended sticks representing the earth's axis and the use of six colours suggesting the global nature of the tournament. The trophy was a two-foot high elongation, as it were, of the logo, the top featuring red and blue prominently, the body silver without inscription or engraving anywhere. The logo was created in house, by David Haney and Joe Bosack of NHL Creative Services.

GENESIS

While the tournament was obviously a modern version of the Canada Cup, the NHL strove to make it an overtly different tournament from its predecessor. Most important, it consisted of two pools, one a European group that played its preliminary games overseas, the other a North American group that played in both Canada and the United States. It also utilized NHL rules and referees.

FIRST WINNER

Team USA won its first prestigious international hockey tournament since the Miracle on Ice in 1980 by beating Canada in three games, but the best-of-three finals was not without controversy. Canada won game one in overtime on a winning goal by Steve Yzerman that was clearly offside, and then in the final minutes of the deciding game the Americans scored the game winner off a Brett Hull deflection that was clearly a high stick. Nonetheless, the Americans went through the tournament with only one loss and, oddly, winning four of their six games by the score of 5-2. In the preliminary round robin they beat Canada 5-3, Russia 5-2, and Slovakia 9-3 to finish first in the North American pool. They advanced to the finals with another 5-2 win over Russia while Canada beat Sweden 3-2 in overtime in the other semi-finals to set up an all-North American finals. It was the pinnacle of achievement for that generation of American player which included Mike Modano, Chris Chelios, Keith Tkachuk, Mike Richter, and Derian Hatcher. Some 15 players from this team played for the USA at the 2002 Olympics in Salt Lake City where they won silver to Canada's gold.

CHAMPIONS' HISTORY

Team Canada won the first Canada Cup in 1976 on a dramatic overtime goal from Darryl Sittler, but it lost to the Soviets five years later by a lop-sided 8-1 score at the Forum in Montreal. Canada won again in 1984 and 1987, the latter perhaps the most exciting of any of the Canada Cups, and in 1991 the victory over the U.S. foreshadowed the emerging American team. Canada swept that best-of-three in two games, but the core of that group of players went on to win the '96 World Cup, the intervening five years providing opportunity for young or inexperienced stars such as Mike Modano and Keith Tkachuk to reach maturity. The 2004 World Cup was re-claimed by Canada with a dramatic 3-2 win over Finland in a finals played at Air Canada Centre in Toronto. Borje Salming, who played for Sweden in the 1976 Canada Cup, presented the Frank Gehry-designed trophy to captain Mario Lemieux following the win (see pages 144-145).

TODAY

The World Cup of Hockey trophy for 1996 did not last very long. Public sentiment called it unpopular and it was shelved for the 2004 World Cup. The 1996 version is on permanent display at the Hockey Hall of Fame.

A dramatic perspective of the top of the trophy featuring the steel body and the two primary colours depicting hockey players.

At the time, the 1996 World Cup trophy was as modern as hockey trophy design got. For the victorious American team, the tournament marked the pinnacle of success for a generation of players that included Brett Hull, Doug Weight, Chris Chelios, and Keith Tkachuk.

1998 SPENGLER CUP

THE TROPHY

Another unique gem, this Spengler Cup was a one-time trophy for the 1998 winner. Made of a glass compound, it has a clear base under which sits a wood one. The body of the trophy consists of five upturned hockey sticks, the blades holding a globe on which is engraved the tournament name. Team Canada received the trophy and got to take it home, a new one crafted for the 1999 tournament.

WINNER

The five teams each played every other team once in a round robin, the top two teams in the standings advancing to the championship game. In 1998, the home team, HC Davos, finished in first place with a 3-1-0 record, their only loss a 5-4 decision to Farjestad of Sweden. Canada also finished with a 3-1-0 record but was placed second because the team's only loss was to Davos, 5-1, to close out the round robin games. In the final game of the tournament, Canada reversed the outcome, beating the home side 5-2 in the traditional New Year's Eve finale. The Canadians jumped out to a 3-0 lead before the game was 12 minutes old, but two goals by Reto Von Arx in the second brought the score close for the home side. Canada's Daniel Marois scored before the second period had ended, however, and Mario Doyon gave Canada some insurance with the final goal in the third. It was the country's fourth straight Spengler victory, and for their dynastic run they were given the trophy. Three members of that team made it to the tournament all-star team: goalie Fred Brathwaite and forwards Dan Hodgson and Jean-Yves Roy. Because the Spengler is both a team and international tournament there are often players from the same country competing against each other. Shayne Wright, for instance, a member of this 1998 team and a native of Welland, Ontario, played for USA two years previous because that country sent the Rochester Americans of the AHL as its representatives, and Wright was on that team during that season. The rest of Team Canada was a universal mix of players who were playing in Europe at the time (Shawn Heaphy, Dave McLlwain, Adrien Plavsic, Hodgson); players from the minors in North America (Shawn Heins, Marty Murray, Brathwaite, and Wright); players from Canadian junior (Geoff Peters, Jeremy Adduono); the National Team (the ever-present Chris Szysky, Bob Maudie); and a backup goalie playing U.S. College (Aaron Schweitzer). The head coach was Mike Johnston. Other teams also featured recognizable names from the pro ranks. In fact, the losing goalie in the final game was none other than Canadian Stephane Beauregard who had 90 games to his NHL record and who had left the IHL to sign with Davos just this season. Davos also had Finnish defenceman Petteri Nummelin, Swede Tommy Sjodin, and American Chris Tancill. The Czech team, HC Slovnaft Vsetin had Roman Cechmanek in goal and Jiri Dopita up front. The Austrians (VEU Feldkirch) had four Canadians on their roster and their own Reinhard Divis in goal, and the Swedes had an impressive lineup that included Kristian Huselius, Jorgen Jonsson, and Peter Nordstrom.

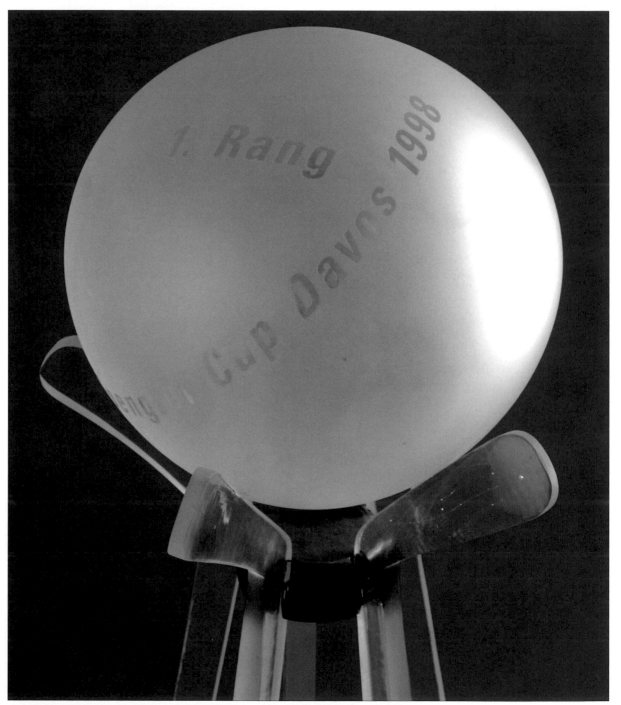

An up-close look at the planetarium-like globe that rests on five hockey sticks.

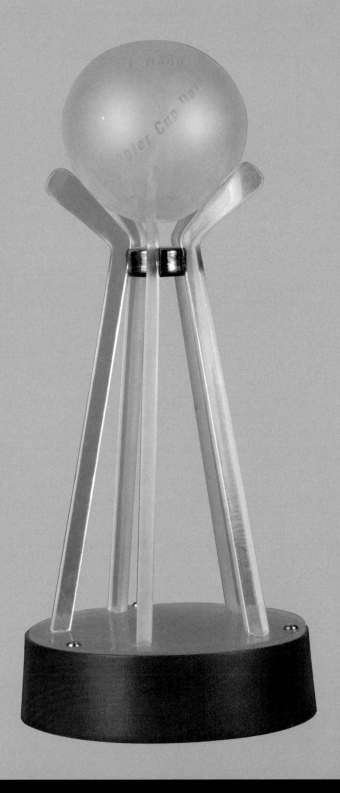

The Spengler Cup has a tradition of trophy design that is as rich as the tournament itself, and the Hockey Hall of Fame has a spectacular collection of that history. This version, for the 1998 winner, Canada, featured a wood base, five hockey sticks, and an inscribed, frosted globe.

MAURICE "ROCKET" RICHARD TROPHY

1998-PRESENT

THE NAME

Maurice Richard was the legendary right winger of the Montreal Canadiens who retired in 1960 after having scored 544 goals, tops in NHL history to that point. He was the first to score 50 goals in a season, and 50 in 50 games (1944-45), and the "fiery eyes" of #9 were the stuff of legend.

THE TROPHY

The top half of the trophy features a two-part curtain that gives the feel of an arena, and the central image is a gold sculpture of Richard skating with the puck. The base of the top has the Canadiens' logo. The bottom half of the trophy is made of wood. The sides are filled with small plaques, two with vignettes of the Montreal Forum and others with dedications. Appropriately, the trophy can accommodate 50 winners' names.

GENESIS

Gord Miller and Bob McKenzie of broadcaster The Sports Network (TSN) mooted the idea on national television in 1998 of introducing a trophy for the league's top goal scorer, and within a year the design team of Sylvie Beauchesne and Jean-Raymond Goyer of Montreal had come up with the league's newest trophy, to honour the player each season who scores the greatest number of goals.

FIRST WINNER

By the time the first winner of the Maurice Richard Trophy had been decided in 1999, Richard himself was close to death. Still, he attended the NHL Awards Dinner in Toronto that June and appeared on stage to hand his trophy over to

its first winner, Teemu Selanne of Anaheim, who led the 27-team NHL in goals scored with 47. Rarely has there been such emotion on stage at the ceremonies and rarely has a man received an ovation such as the one the Rocket received as he came out to give Selanne the trophy.

CHAMPIONS' HISTORY

Appropriately, Pavel Bure, the Russian Rocket, won the trophy in 1999-2000 and 2000-01 when he led the league with years of 58 and 59 goals, respectively, playing for the Florida Panthers. These were the first years of the award after Richard passed away in May 2000. The year after, Milan Hejduk of Colorado was the only player in the league to score 50. In 2003-04, there was an historic three-way tie for the trophy and with no tie-break formula the NHL gave a miniature version to all of Rick Nash (Columbus), Jarome Iginla (Calgary), and Ilya Kovalchuk (Atlanta). The league had had preliminary discussions to have a tie-breaking formula and considered a number of options: (a) the player who had played the fewest games; (b) the player with the most total points; (c) the man with the fewest empty-net goals. In the end, all three have their name on the trophy for the '03-'04 season. Incredibly, Nash, at 19 years and 10 months of age, was some 14 months younger than Wayne Gretzky to lead the league in scoring, the youngest ever. Iginla won his one-third of glory by scoring a goal on the final day of the season.

TODAY

The Richard Trophy has quickly become an integral part of the Hockey Hall of Fame's NHL trophies display in the Great Hall. The excitement for the award indicates how long overdue it was, but it is also a reaction to its winners, who have been mostly younger stars in the game. When Bure won in 1999-2000 and 2000-01, he was 29 and 30 years old, respectively, the oldest player to win so far (Selanne was 28, Hejduk 27, Iginla 24 when he won the first time, and Kovalchuk just 21).

(left) Details from the uppermost base depicting the Forum, a Richard quote, and the commemorative plaque; (above) the Rocket from above; (right) the Rocket from behind, as many a player saw him.

The newest trophy in the NHL's showcase, the Rocket Richard Trophy
honours goal scoring, plain and simple. Gordie Howe and Wayne
Gretzky may have scored more times in their careers, but Richard set
the benchmark in 1944-45 when he scored 50 goals in 50 games.

CHAMPIONSHIP CUP

1999-PRESENT

THE NAME

The Championship Cup is the top prize awarded to the winners of the National Women's Hockey League, the only full-time women's league in the world.

THE TROPHY

As an unlikely a symbol of women's hockey superiority, the Championship Cup is unique if nothing else. The wood base holds the trophy's name on a special brown plaque, and the large barrel containing the names of all winning players each year is outdone only by the even larger vessel above it. The barrel is perfectly round and of one piece, unlike the Stanley Cup which has five barrel rings. Like the Stanley Cup, however, this trophy has every winning player's name engraved on it. The large bowl at the top looks like a challenging object from which to drink champagne, but the overall effect is, without doubt, one of a championship trophy.

GENESIS

The meteoric rise of women's hockey in the 1990s culminated with the establishing of a women's hockey league in 1999 as a means of legitimizing the sport in professional terms and providing a true league in which women can earn a living and develop their talents while looking at the Olympics and World Championships as the pinnacle of their seasons and careers. The first world championship tournament took place in 1989 in Toronto, and a year later the first, fully-sanctioned IIHF championship took place. Women's hockey received its greatest boost when the IOC made it a full Olympic event for the 1998 games in Nagano, Japan, and in the 21st century the world championship is now an annual event. However, the NWHL filled an important gap because formerly women had few options to play on a regular basis. Some chose the U.S. college route, but since many of the top players were Canadian and many of post-college age, they needed a league to call their own. The NWHL continues to exist and thrive, and it is able to provide high-calibre hockey not only for Canadians and Americans but also Finns and Swedes and emerging European players. It is the best women's league for developing the game and promoting growth both at the player and fan levels.

FIRST WINNER

The Beatrice Aeros were the first NWHL champions by virtue of their two-game finals victory over Sainte-Julie Pantheres. On March 18, 2000, they played to a 2-2 tie, and the next night the Aeros won 1-0 to win the series three points to one. In 1999-2000, the NWHL featured nine teams in two divisions: the East consisted of four teams (Montreal Wingstar, Ottawa Raiders, Laval Le Mistral, and the Pantheres, who finished first in their division to earn a place in the finals); the West had five teams (Brampton Thunder, Mississauga Chiefs, Clearnet Lightning, Scarborough Sting, and the Aeros, who were first in their division). The East played 35 games and the West 40 games during the regular schedule, and the top team from each advanced to the Championship Cup finals. The Aeros featured a who's who of World Championship and Olympic gold medalists: Cassie Campbell, Cherie Piper, Angela James, Geraldine Heaney, Cheryl Pounder. The Pantheres were a mostly French-Canadian team with an impressive lineup of their own led by Nancy Drolet. Drolet was the hero in game one of the finals, scoring in the final minute to give the Pantheres the tie. In game two, Piper was the hero, scoring the only goal of the game, in the first period, enough to give the Aeros the win and the first NWHL championship.

CHAMPIONS' HISTORY

The Aeros won the Championship Cup each of the first three years, beating the Pantheres again in 2001 and the Brampton Thunder at the end of the 2001-02 season. The Calgary X-Treme, in the west, ended the Aeros' run, beating them in the 2003 finals, and the X-Treme repeated as champs in 2004, beating the Thunder this time. In 2004-05, the Toronto Aeros won again, defeating the Montreal Axion.

TODAY

Although the Championship Cup is on display at the Hockey Hall of Fame, like the Stanley Cup, it is still very much active and every spring is awarded to the NWHL league champions.

(left) Dedication plaque at the base of the trophy; *(above)* the winning names inscribed for the 2002-03 season.

The Stanley Cup of women's hockey, the Championship Cup is given to the playoff winner from the National Women's Hockey League, a burgeoning, necessary league that showcases most Canadian Olympians and many Americans as well.

2004 WORLD CUP OF HOCKEY TROPHY

2004

THE NAME

The World Cup of Hockey was a tournament first played in 1996 to replace the Canada Cup, a pioneering competition created by deposed player agent Alan Eagleson in 1976 to showcase the best players from the top hockey countries, regardless whether professional or amateur.

THE TROPHY

The 2004 World Cup trophy consists of two tiers of warped, ice-like plastic atop which sits a removable cup made of copper and nickel alloy. This cup will have the players' names from the winning team engraved on it and preserved at the Hall of Fame. The plastic below is virtually unbreakable, so players can hold it high (it weighs 23.5 pounds) and drop it without fear, a factor architect and designer Frank Gehry considered when choosing materials. "The light catches the trophy the same way it catches ice," Gehry said at the unveiling. "Ice was the metaphor here. I thought it should evoke ice and hockey, and north, not south," he explained. For the next World Cup, a new cup will be installed at the top and the engraving process repeated.

GENESIS

The 1972 Summit Series was the most important hockey series ever played. It featured the best players from Canada (NHL stars) against the best from the Soviet Union (league players) in an eight-game showdown, the first four games played in Canada (Montreal, Toronto, Winnipeg, Vancouver) and the last four in Moscow (Luzhniki Arena). The high quality of play, the drama, and the political importance of the series was highlighted by the grit and determination of Canada against the rococo style of offense of the Soviets, a clash of methods, values, and systems that climaxed with Paul Henderson's heroic series winner in the final minute of the final game. As a result of the success of this series, NHLPA executive director Alan Eagleson organized a six-nation tournament for September 1976 in which the best played the best for the first time. When Eagleson confessed to various hockey-related crimes in a Boston courtroom and was ousted from the league and the Hockey Hall of Fame, the NHL reconstituted the tournament under the more neutral aegis of the World Cup. The first World Cup was held in 1996, but it came under fire for introducing an aesthetically unpopular trophy that few fans seemed to like. For 2004, the NHL did what seemed to make perfect sense: it hired world famous architect and Toronto-born hockey fan Frank Gehry to design a new trophy for 2004. The result was an even more perplexing and enigmatic vessel that caused many a curious look when Gehry presented it to the press on May 12, 2004, at the Hockey Hall of Fame.

FIRST WINNER

Canada defeated Finland 3-2 in the one-game finals at Air Canada Centre, Toronto, the night before the NHL's collective bargaining agreement with the players expired and threw the league into a state of distress. The tournament victory was a continuation of Canadian dominance in world competition and confirmed a renaissance of the country's supremacy that has also been augmented by gold medals for men and women at the 2002 Olympics, gold for men and women at the World Championships in 2004, and gold for Canada's national junior team in January 2005.

CHAMPIONS' HISTORY

Although the USA defeated Canada in three games in 1996 and the Soviets won the Canada Cup in 1981, Canada is the only country to appear in every finals and was the victor in all other years: 1976, 1984, 1987, and 1991.

TODAY

The Gehry trophy remains in the Hockey Hall of Fame, on display and waiting for a new tournament to be organized, though this likely won't happen until 2008 so as not to conflict with the 2006 Olympic Winter Games in Turin, Italy.

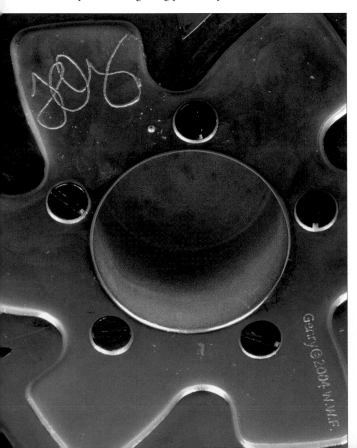

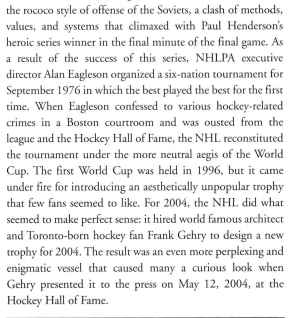

(far left) The underside of the trophy, signed by Frank Gehry; (top) the name as it appears on one part of the plastic underside; (near left) the top of the bowl as it fits in with the plastic body.

If you're going to get an architect to design a hockey trophy, it might as well be the greatest living architect (Frank Gehry) who also happens to have lived his childhood in hockey-mad Toronto. The result is this utterly unique trophy won by Canada in September 2004.

JACK RILEY CUP
EAST COAST HOCKEY LEAGUE

1988-89 CAROLINA THUNDERBIRDS
1989-90 GREENSBORO MONARCHS
1990-91 HAMPTON ROADS ADMIRALS
1991-92 HAMPTON ROADS ADMIRALS
1992-93 TOLEDO STORM
1993-94 TOLEDO STORM
1994-95 RICHMOND RENEGADES
1995-96 CHARLOTTE CHECKERS

HOBEY BAKER MEMORIAL AWARD
PRESENTED ANNUALLY TO THE OUTSTANDING COLLEGIATE HOCKEY PLAYER
IN THE UNITED STATES BY THE
DECATHLON ATHLETIC CLUB OF BLOOMINGTON, MINNESOTA

THE EDINBURGH TROPHY

Gallery

CANADIAN AMATEUR HOCKEY
LEAGUE TROPHY
(1899-1905)

PATTON CUP
(1914-PRESENT)

One of the oldest hockey trophies, the Canadian Amateur Hockey League championship trophy was around only six seasons. The first winners were the Shamrocks of Montreal which won again the next year. Ottawa, Montreal, and Quebec won in succeeding years, and the last winners were the Victoria Hockey Club of Montreal in 1905.

In circulation since 1914, the T.B. Patton Cup is awarded to the Western Canadian champions of senior hockey. The first winners were the Regina Victorias in 1913-14, but the most famous of early winners were the Winnipeg Falcons of 1919-20 that went on to win gold for Canada at the 1920 Olympics.

ABBOTT CUP
(1918-1999)

Captain E.L. "Hick" Abbott was a star hockey player in the west as a youth. He led the Regina Victorias to national junior championships in 1913 and 1914 and soon after perished in active combat in World War I. In 1919, the Saskatchewan Minor Hockey Association donated this trophy to be presented annually to the champion junior team in western Canada.

QAHA TROPHY
(1930-1960)

The Quebec Amateur Hockey Association named its championship trophy simply after the league name. Donated by Alcide Gagnon and A.T. Love in 1930, this trophy was in annual competition for 30 years to honour the best team in the province in the juvenile age group.

TROPHY TO ROY CONACHER
(1933)

SUTHERLAND CUP
(1934-PRESENT)

Like any Toronto boy who took his hockey seriously, Roy Conacher played in the Toronto Hockey League (THL) before playing junior. He won this trophy with the Marlboros, one of many teams at many levels so named. Conacher went on to have a Hall of Fame career from 1938 to 1952 with three teams, winning the Stanley Cup with the Bruins in 1939 and 1941.

The Sutherland Cup honoured Junior B champions in Ontario. The first winners, in 1934, were the St. Michael's Buzzers, players from which would graduate to play for the Junior A St. Michael's Majors. The winners for 2004-05 were the Thorold Blackhawks.

LESTER PATRICK CUP
(1952-1974)

HART MEMORIAL TROPHY
(1960-PRESENT)

To the champions of the WHL playoffs went the spoils known as the Lester Patrick Cup. The Saskatoon Quakers of 1952-53 were the first winners but it wasn't until 1963-65 that a team won the Patrick Cup in consecutive years, a feat achieved then by the San Francisco Seals. In the early 1970s the Phoenix Roadrunners won consecutively, in 1972-73 and '73-'74, the last year of competition for the trophy.

Introduced in 1960 after the original was retired, the new Hart Trophy looked nothing like its predecessor. Resembling a bulb or flower, the new version has a long stem that sits on a base which holds winners' names. The 2004-05 winner was Martin St. Louis of Tampa Bay, who had an extraordinary year, also winning the Art Ross Trophy, Lester B. Pearson Award, and the Stanley Cup.

HARDY TROPHY
(1968-90)

ORIGINAL CENTENNIAL CUP
(1971-1993)

Canadian-born George Hardy was the president of the IIHF from 1948 to 1951. It was not until the 1967-68 season that a CAHA-sanctioned national intermediate championship was held in Canada. To honour the beginning of this tournament, a group of realtors in North Battleford, Saskatchewan, presented the CAHA with the Hardy Trophy in the name of Edmontonian George Hardy, a life member of the CAHA.

The first version of the Centennial Cup was introduced in 1970 and was given to the provincial Junior A champions of Canada. It was later replaced by a second version, then a third (see pages 92-93) and finally replaced altogether by the Royal Bank Cup in 1995.

1986 IZVESTIA

This was the second-place trophy given to Canada at the 1986 Izvestia tournament in Moscow. Held annually from 1967 to 1997 and named after a newspaper, Izvestia, the tournament was usually held in December just before Christmas. Canada had Zarley Zalapski on defence who was named the tournament's best defenceman.

1991 SPENGLER CUP
(1991-1994)

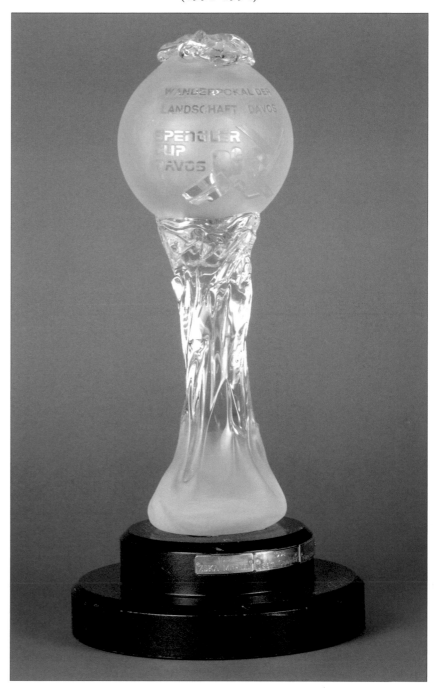

Part old, part new, this Spengler Cup features a modern glass sculpture on an old wood base. The base has small plaques with winning teams' names from 1991 to 1994: "1991 ZSKA Moskau"; "1992 Team Canada"; "1993 Farjestads BK"; "1994 Farjestads BK."

ACKNOWLEDGEMENTS AND PHOTO CREDITS

ACKNOWLEDGEMENTS

The most important thanks goes, first and foremost, to the many people over the years and decades who have preserved the trophies in this book and ensured their safe arrival at the Hockey Hall of Fame. Their donations, their devotion to the game, their belief that these trophies belong at the Hall, all help make it the world's foremost repository of hockey trophies in the world.

The author would like to thank everyone at the Hockey Hall of Fame for contributing in one way or another to making this book a reality: president Jeff Denomme, chairman Bill Hay, and the entire staff, notably Kelly Masse, Craig Baines, Phil Pritchard (for supporting the concept from day one), Craig Campbell (for advice and trophy carrying, especially the 95-pound Canada Cup), Pearl Rajwanth, Anthony Fusco (IT guru), Konrad Jagla's father, Peter, Ron Ellis (#6), Steve Ozimec, Steve Poirier, Danielle Siciliano (for a little bit of everything), Miragh Addis, Izak Westgate (for minor pro and amateur hockey information, trophy carrying, and editing), Tyler (metal man) Wolosewich, Kevin Shea (for editing and proofreading with a keen eye), Darren Boyko (Manitoba Sports Hall of Fame), Jackie Schwartz, Mike Gouglas (IT guru II), Marilyn Robbins (for so much for so long), Sylvia Lau, Sandra Walters, Ray Paquet, Craig Beckim, Wendy Cramer, Tome Geneski, Joanne Laird, Patrick Minogue, Dave Stubbs.

Additionally, the author wishes to thank publisher Jordan Fenn for unwavering support, designer Kathryn Del Borrello for making the pages look seamless and perfect, agent Dean Cooke and his staff, Samantha North and Suzanne Brandreth. And to family (Liz, Ian, Emily, Zachary, mom) and friends (Jon, Joan, Cathy, Mary Jane) for keeping things fun and interesting off ice, as it were.

PHOTO CREDITS

All images in this book were produced by the extraordinary team of James McCrorie and Dennis Miles of Ryerson University. Their makeshift studio was the Founders' Room of the Hockey Hall of Fame, and all trophies are part of the Hockey Hall of Fame's collection.

HOBEY BAKER MEMORIAL AWARD
PRESENTED ANNUALLY TO THE OUTSTANDING COLLEGIATE HOCKEY PLAYER
IN THE UNITED STATES BY THE
DECATHLON ATHLETIC CLUB OF BLOOMINGTON, MINNESOTA